Cloud-hidden,
Whereabouts Unknown

ALSO BY ALAN WATTS

Cloud-hidden, Whereabouts Unknown

A Mountain Journal

ALAN WATTS

PANTHEON BOOKS

A Division of Random House, New York

Copyright © 1968, 1970, 1971, 1973 by Alan Watts

All rights reserved under International and Pan-American Copyright Conventions. Published in the United States by Pantheon Books, a division of Random House, Inc., New York, and simultaneously in Canada by Random House of Canada Limited, Toronto.

Portions of this book were first published in *Mademoiselle, Playboy,* and *Earth.*

Grateful acknowledgment is made to the following:

Lin Yutang, for permission to use his translation of Chia Tao's poem "Searching for the Hermit in Vain," from *My Country and My People,* published by John Day Company.

Miss Dorothy E. Collins and Dodd, Mead & Company, for permission to quote from "The Song of Quoodle," taken from *The Collected Poems of G. K. Chesterton.*

Library of Congress Cataloging in Publication Data

Watts, Alan Wilson, 1915–
Cloud-hidden, Whereabouts Unknown.

   1. Religion—Addresses, essays, lectures.
I. Title.
BL50.W32 1973   200'.1   72–12384
ISBN 0–394–48253–0

Manufactured in the United States of America
by Halliday Lithograph Corp.
West Hanover, Massachusetts

3 5 7 9 8 6 4 2

FIRST EDITION

To Sandy Jacobs

SEARCHING FOR THE HERMIT IN VAIN

I asked the boy beneath the pines.
He said, "The master's gone alone
Herb-picking somewhere on the mount,
Cloud-hidden, whereabouts unknown."

Chia Tao (777–841)
Trans. Lin Yutang

The poem on the preceding page, by Chia Tao of the T'ang dynasty, suits my mood and provides the title of this book. I live between two places—a ferryboat on the Sausalito waterfront and a lonely cottage in the foothills of Mount Tamalpais, just north of San Francisco; a mountain sacred to the Indians which wraps itself in an atmosphere of strange beneficence. During the past three years I have done almost all my writing in this cottage. This includes my recently published autobiography, *In My Own Way,* and a considerable number of short pieces written for my *Journal* (published for subscribers), and for such magazines as *Playboy* and *Earth.* Most of the latter are assembled here in the form of a journal with dated entries, though they are ordered by content rather than chronology because my thinking spirals: it does not go ahead in a straight line.

Some critics will therefore call me repetitious, but I have found, in the process of teaching, that most students do not understand one's ideas unless they are repeated—under differing analogies or in varying forms of words, as a musician constructs variations on a theme. Besides, what I mean by understanding is not simply verbal comprehension: it is feeling it in your bones.

The form of this book is therefore that of a "mountain journal" concerned with the philosophy of nature, ecology, aesthetics, religion, and metaphysics, and the entries are grouped more or less according to those topics. The dates will allow those who are chronologically oriented to rearrange them in their mind's eye.

ALAN WATTS

Druid Heights, California
Spring 1972

Contents

Cloud-hidden,
Whereabouts Unknown

Ever since I can remember anything at all, the light,
the smell, the sound, and motion of the sea have been
pure magic. Even the mere intimation of its presence
—gulls flying a little way inland, the quality of light
in the sky beyond hills which screen it from view, the
lowing of foghorns in the night. If ever I have to get
away from it all, and in the words of the Chinese poet
"wash all the wrongs of life from my pores," there is
simply nothing better than to climb out onto a rock,
and sit for hours with nothing in sight but sea and
sky. Although the rhythm of the waves beats a kind
of time, it is not clock or calendar time. It has no
urgency. It happens to be timeless time. I know that I
am listening to a rhythm which has been just the same
for millions of years, and it takes me out of a world of
relentlessly ticking clocks. Clocks for some reason or
other always seem to be marching, and, as with
armies, marching is never to anything but doom. But
in the motion of waves there is no marching rhythm.
It harmonizes with our very breathing. It does not
count our days. Its pulse is not in the stingy spirit of

The Water

measuring, of marking out how much still remains. It is the breathing of eternity, like the God Brahma of Indian mythology inhaling and exhaling, manifesting and dissolving the worlds, forever. As a mere conception this might sound appallingly monotonous, until you come to listen to the breaking and washing of waves.

Thus, I have come to live right on the edge of the water. I have a studio, library, a place for writing on an old ferryboat tied up on the waterfront of Sausalito, north of San Francisco. I suppose this place is the nearest thing in America to a Mediterranean fishing village. Steep hills clustered with little houses, and below along the rim of the bay a forest of masts rocking almost imperceptibly against a background of water and wooded promontories. In some ways this is a rather messy waterfront, not just piers and boats, but junkyards, industrial buildings, and all the inevitable "litter-ature" of our culture. But somehow the land-and-seascape absorbs and pacifies the mess. Sheds and shacks thrown together out of old timbers and plywood, heaps of disused lumber, rusted machinery, and rotting hulls—all of this is transformed in the beneficent presence of the sea.

Perhaps it is the quality of the light, especially early in the morning and towards evening, when the distinction between sky and water becomes uncertain, when the whole of space becomes opalescent in a sort of pearly luminous grey, and when the rising or setting moon is straw yellow. In this light all the rambling mess of sheds and junkyards is magical, blessed with the patterns of masts and ropes and boats at anchor. It all puts me in mind of landfalls a long way off, and all the voyages one has dreamed of.

I look out now across a wide space of nothing but water

and birds ending in a line of green slopes with clumps of trees. Right over the edge of the boat the water contains seemingly just under the surface a ceaselessly moving network of reflected sunlight through which a school of very tiny fish passes delightfully uncaught. Yet only a few yards from where we are moored, tackle shops sell the salmon and crabs with which this particular area abounds.

This is the paradox of the ocean. Sand, flying spray, pebbles and shells, driftwood, sparkling water, space incredibly luminous with cloudbanks along horizons underlying skies into which one's imagination can reach without end. But under the surface of both sky and water there is the grim business of preying. Men and birds against fish, fish against fish. The tortuous process of life continuing by the painful transformation of one form or body into another. To creatures who do not anticipate and reflect imaginatively on this holocaust of eating and being eaten, this is perhaps not so terrible. But poor man! Skillful beyond all other animals, by being able to think in time, and abstractly knowing the future, he dies before he is dead. He shrinks from the shark's teeth before they bite him, and he dreads the alien germ long, long before its banquet begins.

At this moment I see a gull that has picked a crab from a tidepool. Sprawled now upon the sand, the crab shrinks from the walls of its shell which is resounding to the tap, tap, tap of the gull's beak. Who's that knocking at my door?

I suppose the shell of a crab, a clam, or a mussel is the boundary of its universe. To put ourselves into their position, we would have to imagine a knocking sound louder and louder, a sound which doesn't come from anywhere in particular, from some door, the walls, the ceiling, the floor.

No, instead think of a knocking which comes from every-where, beating against all the boundaries of space and consciousness, intruding like some utterly unknown dimension into our known and familiar world.

"Let me in! Let me in! I love you so much I could eat you. I love you to the very core, especially the soft, juicy parts, the vitals most tender and alive. Surrender to this agony, and you will be transformed into Me. Dying to your-self you will become alive as Me. We shall all be changed in a moment, in the twinkling of an eye, on the morning when the last trumpet sounds. For behold! I am He who stands at the door and knocks."

There is simply no way of getting around all this. The gull can't really be said to be rapacious or greedy. It's just that his being alive at all is the same thing as eating crabs. Sea birds are transformations of fish; men are transforma-tions of wheat, steers, and chickens. A love for the food is the very agony of the food. To object to this inseparability of pleasure and pain, life and death, is to object to exist-ence. But, of course, we cannot help objecting when our time comes. *Objecting to pain is pain.* So far as we know, the gull and the fish don't philosophize. They appear instead to enjoy life when they are eating, and hate it when being eaten. But they don't reflect upon the process as a whole and say, "How rough to have to work so hard for a living," or, "It's just hell having to watch out all the time for those damn gulls." I'm sure that in their world this is all some-thing that just goes along with life like having eyes or feet or wings.

But man, with his astonishing ability to stand aside from himself and think about himself—in short, to comment on life, man has done something which confuses his own exist-

6

ence down to its roots. For the more sensitive he is, the more he finds the very act of living in conflict with his moral conscience. Upon reflection a universe so arranged that there is no way of living except by destroying other lives seems to be a hideous mistake, not a divine but a devilish creation. Of course, there is the myth that once upon a time things were quite otherwise, that there was no death, that the lion lay down with the lamb. But that since then there has been a fall, a vast error which has corrupted the whole of nature. But all that must have been eons ago, perhaps in some other galaxy where the conditions of life were quite different. Or perhaps the ghastly mistake was just that step in man's evolution which made it possible for him to reflect, to comment upon life as a whole. For in being able to stand aside from life and think about it, he also put himself outside it and found it alien. Perhaps thinking about the world and objecting to its whole principle are simply two aspects of but one activity. The very words suggest, do they not, that *we must object to everything that becomes an object*? But aren't there also times when we speak of something that we know as a *subject*— the subject of this book, the subject I am now studying. I wonder, then, *would it be possible to subject to life instead of objecting to it*? Is this merely playing with words, or does it possibly mean something?

Now, if the gulls and the fish do not philosophize, they have no consciousness of life being good as a whole or bad as a whole. So when we philosophize and pity the poor fish, that really turns out to be just our own problem. From its own standpoint, the world of plants and animals and insects and birds does not find itself problematic at all. There isn't the slightest evidence to suggest such dis-ease.

7

On the contrary, I incline to feel that all these creatures really "swing" or "groove." They go on living right up to the very moment when the game is no longer worth the candle. I'm quite sure that they don't lecture each other about their duties or worry about where they are going after they die.

Isn't it, then, an enormous relief for us men to see that the plant and animal world is not a problem to itself, and that we are wasting intellectual energy in making moral judgments about it? But, of course, we can't return to the unreflective consciousness of the animal world without becoming monstrous in a way that animals are not. To be human is precisely to have that extra circuit of consciousness which enables us to know that we know, and thus to take an attitude towards all that we experience. The mistake which we have made—and this, if anything, *is the fall of man*—is to suppose that that extra circuit, that ability to take an attitude toward the rest of life as a whole, is the same as actually standing aside and being separate from what we see. We seem to feel that the thing which knows that it knows is one's essential self, that—in other words— our personal identity is entirely on the side of the commentator. We forget, because we learn to ignore so subtly, the larger organismic fact that self-consciousness is simply a subordinate part and an instrument of our whole being, a sort of mental counterpart of the finger-thumb opposition in the human hand. Now which is really you, the finger or the thumb?

Observe the stages of this differentiation, the levels of abstraction: First, the organism from its environment, and with this knowledge of the environment. Second, the distinction of knowing knowledge from knowledge itself. But in concrete fact all this, like the finger-thumb opposition, is a *difference which does not divide*. The thumb is not floating in the air alongside the rest of the hand. At their roots both fingers and thumb are joined. And at our roots we are joined to the whole subject of nature. Of course, you might say that nature or the whole universe is nothing but a big abstraction. But tell me, is an orange nothing but an abstraction from its component molecules, skins, segments, fibers and fluids?

I think that our difficulty is we have learned to feel our consciousness much too superficially, as if all our sensation were in the tips of the fingers and none in the palm. Our comments on life are insufficiently balanced by the clear sensation that *what we are talking about is ourselves*, and ourselves in a sense far more basic and real than that extra circuit which knows knowing. Are we misled by the fact that we move freely on the earth and are not rooted to it in the same way as trees to the ground or fingers to the hand? Were we as spatially distant from the earth as one atom of an orange from another, I suppose we might be somewhere out by the moon or Mars. Now we know that the atom, the molecule, the cell, or subordinate organ of any particular organism is what it is by virtue of its place and its membership in the pattern of the whole. But blood in a test tube rapidly ceases to be the same thing as blood in veins. In the same way, man must beware (be + aware) lest in cutting himself off psychically from the world which he sees, and so isolating the subject from the object, lest in doing this he rapidly ceases to be man.

So I think this is why I love the ocean. It is the most difficult part of nature to mess up with emblems and symptoms of man's dissociated consciousness, though by no means impossible to nationalistic, industrial man. But the ocean is an environment in which *the awareness of our roots can awaken,* in which space so real because of the light and color can be seen as joining things instead of separating them.

And, oh yes, I have just discovered that that knocking on the walls of all space and consciousness is my own heart beating.

August 1970

There is the water, and now there is also the mountain. (In Chinese the two characters for "mountain" and "water" mean "landscape.") I have the use of a small one-room cottage on the slopes of the mountain —Tamalpais—which I can see from the ferryboat. It is hidden in a grove of high eucalyptus trees and overlooks a long valley whose far side is covered with a dense forest of bay, oak, and madrone so even in height that from a distance it looks like brush. No human dwelling is in view, and the principal inhabitant of the forest is a wild she-goat who has been there for at least nine years. Every now and then she comes out and dances upon the crown of an immense rock which rises far out of the forest. No one goes to this forest. I have been down to its edge, where there is a meadow, good for practicing archery, and I think that one of these days I will explore the forest. But then again I may not, for there are places which people should leave alone.

In these days of overpopulation and social evils crying for concern it may seem wicked to withdraw

And the
Mountain

11

from the crowd—even from the bohemian and hippie crowd of the Sausalito waterfront. But, to tell the truth, I have some—but little—faith in the historical idealism of "human progress." Like the planet itself, human history goes round. There are dawns of hope and sunsets of sorrow, springs of aspiration and autumns of despair, even though one's attitude can so be changed that one sees in autumn the beginning of a cycle whose end is spring. This is not saying, "To hell with people!"—as if I were somehow superior to the common man, a term which actually means the Man common to us all and thus (if I may be forgiven a pun in Sanskrit) the *atman*, our supra-individual Self.

There are situations when one *owes* solitude to other people, if only not to bother them. But, more than this, the multitude needs solitaries as it needs postmen, doctors, and fishermen. They go out and they send, or bring, something back—even if they send no word and vanish finally from sight. The solitary is as necessary to our common sanity as wilderness, as the forest where no one goes, as the waterfall in a canyon which no one has ever seen or heard. We do not *see* our hearts. I do not expect to be all that solitary for, as a paradoxical person, I am also gregarious and favor the rhythm of withdrawal and return. But in the mountain I watch the Tao, the way of nonhuman nature (if there is really any such thing) and feel myself into it to discover that I was never outside, because nature "peoples" just as much as it "forests."

To realize this one must go beyond what both distinguishes and segregates us as human beings—our thoughts and ideas. To put it in a rather extreme way: We are misled when we believe that our ideas represent or mirror nature, because that sets us outside nature as mere observ-

12

ers. The tree does not represent the fish, though both use light and water. The point is rather that our thoughts and ideas *are* nature, just as much as waves on the ocean and clouds in the sky. The mind grows thoughts as the field grows grass. If I think about thoughts, as if there were some "I," some thinker watching them from outside, there arises the infinite regression of thinking about thinking, etc., because this "I" is itself a thought, and thoughts, like trees, grow of themselves. In solitude it is easier for thoughts to leave themselves alone. It is, thus, a mistake to try to get rid of thoughts, for who will push them out? But when thoughts leave themselves alone the mind clears up.

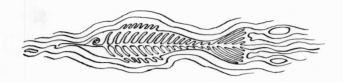

January 25, 1971

After the rains, the mountain stream at the bottom of the valley can be heard all night. It is not pushed from behind, but falls with gravity. Heard from a distance, it sighs; close by, it burbles and chuckles, hisses and gurgles. Whirligigs stay in the same places with very slight variations of pattern, but the water goes on and on.

The Watercourse Way

> The waters before, and the waters after,
> Now and forever flowing, follow each other.

"Panta rhei," said Heraclitus—everything flows, and you cannot step twice into the same stream. The flow of water, of wind, and of fire is obvious, as is also the flow of thought. The flow of earth and rock is less obvious, but in the long run the hard is as liquid as the soft. Streams and waves never stop moving, and yet they are at rest, and restful to hear, because they are in no hurry to reach any destination. Indeed, they are not going anywhere at all.

When I stand by the stream and watch it, I am relatively still, and the flowing water makes a path across my memory so that I realize its transience in compari-

15

son with my stability. This is, of course, an illusion in the sense that I, too, am in flow and likewise have no final destination—for can anyone imagine finality as a form of life? My death will be the disappearance of a particular pattern in the water.

Feeling all that I can possibly feel, aware of every level and dimension of experience, I find nothing but a streaming. If I ask myself *what* is streaming, I cannot imagine an answer even though I have the definite impression that "It" —some energy, some basic gazoozle—is streaming in every kind of stream, streams of rock, streams of light, streams of air, streams of consciousness. This "It" is not different from the streaming and its patterns as clay is different from the shape of this or that particular vessel. It isn't the stuff of which waves are made. There is simply no way of thinking or talking about It, and the significance of this is not so much that there is indeed some unthinkable and transcendental It, but that there is absolutely no way of standing outside It and getting hold of It. It could of course be myself, considered as the relatively enduring center of all my experiences. But if this is so, myself is beyond my reach, and the more I try to pin it down, the more it dissolves into the streaming—into various kinds of pulsing and textures of tensing only arbitrarily distinguishable from the sights and sounds of the world outside me. If this "I" should try to stop the streaming or to manage it all, there is only a futile state of tension without the intended result.

But this particular kind of tension against the stream is habitual, and the frustration which it engenders is chronic. If I believe that I would like to break the habit, that very wish is another form of the same tension, and this in turn is a form of the basic un-get-at-ability of It. We are all lunatics trying to stick pins into their own points, and it is thus that our frantic efforts to set the world to rights and to extend our control over all happenings, inner and outer, are themselves the cause of most of our troubles. All *force* is tension against the stream.

Everywhere there are now people absorbed in projects to change the world or to change themselves, and they will simply perpetuate, or merely change the form, of the very troubles they intend to avoid. This is not to say that human life and conduct is inevitably a tragic mess. It is to say that human life—and all life—does not work harmoniously when we try to force it to be other than what it is, for the very simple reason that this is based on the assumption that I, who would control things, am something apart from what I would control. This assumption is a hallucination supported by the force of almost universal social consensus. You, on the one hand, are responsible for what you do, on the other. To think or feel otherwise is taboo. It is called passivity, inertia, weakness, and spineless fatalism. But the most valuable insights come through questioning the most obvious forms of common sense.

What happens with your stream of experience if you realize that no one is in control of it? If you see that it is just going along of itself, unpushed and unpulled? (This is what the Chinese writing on this page means: The Tao, the course of nature, flows of itself.) You can get the feel of it by breathing without doing anything to help your breath along. Let the breath out, and then let it come back by itself, when it feels like it. And then out again when it wants to go out. Keep this up until you are completely comfortable with letting it go its own way, and you will notice that the rhythm slows down without the least effort—and

17

at the same time becomes a little stronger. This happens because you are now "with" the breath and no longer "outside" it as controller. Something similar happens when you let thoughts, feelings, and all other experiences follow their own course. They are doing this anyhow and you can't really make it otherwise, so if some contrary tension arises see that it, too, is happening of itself—and watch to see what it wants to do. Just watch the stream going along, nothing more. If you find yourself asking who is watching and why, take it as simply another wiggle of the stream.

Our normal expectation is that in such a state as this the stream of events would run wild, and if we cling to this expectation, wild they will be, and this is especially so for those who hold the supposition that to act naturally and spontaneously is to do everything which social convention forbids. But by following the obverse of social convention one is still letting it determine one's pattern of behavior, and the stream is not being asked how *it* would flow— which has nothing to do with accepting or rejecting conventional systems. The almost shocking surprise is that when the stream is not externally controlled it controls itself, automatically, and there is no anxious sensation that it is running away with you. For you *are* this stream, and it was never actually otherwise. Watch, however, how the mind will hatch reason after reason for not making this experiment. This is why so few people ever make it and why there are so few examples of how it works, and consequently so little trust in its feasibility.

It is thus that no creative or constructive action can come to pass without one's first realizing that every willful effort to improve the world or oneself is futile, and so long as one can be beguiled by any political or spiritual scheme for molding things nearer to the heart's desire one will be frustrated, angry, or depressed—that is, unless the first step in any such scheme is to see that nothing can be done. This is not because you are a victim of fate, but because there is no "you" to be fated, no observing self apart from the stream. For when the illusion of the "you" outside and apart from the stream is dissipated, you are in a position of power to work with the stream and not against it. It is as if you had restored your balance in dancing or judo. Real freedom cannot exist alongside false freedom, but the abandonment of false freedom looks as if it would leave you as good as dead. But this is the secret of Goethe's *Stirb und werde*, "Die and come to life." For the job of compassion in a sick society only the dead need apply.

Although we speak of clouds as drifting freely and of streams as flowing freely, this seems to be no more than poetic imagery, for do not clouds obey the wind and water the force of gravity? It is most important to give up our military way of seeing the world as a chain of command—as a handing down of infrangible laws and orders from before to after. It requires a still more startling breach of common sense to see that the present is not governed by the past, and that we shall seek in vain along the backward track of time to discover the determinative origin of the universe. Fine instruments and calculations may restore the track for billions of years, but in the end it will fade out. So there was once a Big Bang . . . and before that? The child knows this intuitively when it asks, "But who made God?" Change the question a little, realizing that God is eternal, and ask, "Who makes God?" You do.

If God is conceived as the superauthority who made the world at the distant beginning of time, he is as much your own fabrication as the notion that you yourself are something other than your stream of experiences. The idea may have been thought up by your remote ancestors, but you bought it. But if you realize that you are not this sad and silly abstract ego trying to run the world from outside, then God is made by quite another kind of "you." This is the "you" that not only makes God but is God—although, to avoid the inevitable military and authoritarian associations of this name, it is better to speak of the Tao, since "the Tao which can be defined is not the eternal Tao."

From this altered standpoint it is easy to see the sense in which you are making the world, or rather, that the world is making itself. As trees evoke sound from the wind, your eyes evoke light from fire. The structure of your organism, of your senses and nerves, endows the world with all its sensible and measurable properties—for rocks cannot seem to be hard except in relation to soft skin. All knowledge, all experience could be said to be a neural situation inside the skull, and the brain is not merely a receiver and recorder of input through the senses: it also has output because the way in which it structures its senses and nerve patterns shapes the input in the same way that a harpist, by selective plucking, brings formal melody out of a row of uniformly scaled and otherwise silent strings. Thus the brain evokes the sensible world by sounding the strings of all those vibrations which we call the real, external world. Every brain plays its own world, but all brains of similar structure are playing similar worlds, and a brain of different structure would make a different selection of vibrations and so evoke from them a world quite different from ours.

But the brain itself is in and of that external world, a particular pattern of vibrations, and the organism as a whole is functionally inseparable from that brain. And, in turn, the organism is functionally inseparable from the environment, from a system of vibrations from which it can make those particular selections which it calls being alive. Thus the subtle environment of this particular planet, solar system, and galaxy grows human organisms as a tree grows fruit. The fruit, in turn, contains the seed of another tree of the same genus. Which came the first, fruit or tree? Imagine the two processes as happening simultaneously—the tree growing the fruit, and the fruit growing the tree—and you will see, by analogy, the brain shaping the environment, and the environment shaping the brain. That is a clumsy way of saying that you are seeing a *single* process. (The organism differs from the environment as one side of a Möbius strip "differs" from the other. Because of a twist or flip in the strip, you can grasp one and the same side between two different fingers.)

This mutual creation of the world, as between organism and environment, is happening *now*. True, there is evidence around—monumental evidence—of a past, of vibrations which have been evoked before, of age-old hills and ancient buildings. Yet these very remains and memories are being reiterated and structured from the vibrations in the present. The Creation, then, is not a unique event in the past, caus-ing and determining all that follows. It is *nowever,* and the past trails behind it inactive and dead, influencing the pres-ent only to the extent that we keep on insisting that it does and should—for we keep reactivating the past in the hope that history is guiding us to where we should be going in the future, and this is driving the car with eyes glued to the rear-vision mirror. And history is the story of our consistent failures in trying to control the stream from without—a monotonous process of self-frustration that will go on and on until we stop trying to force the course and let it flow of itself.

This is not to "look to the future" as that phrase is ordinarily understood, for any future that we know, or think we know, is an extrapolation from the past. The future is unknown. Prophecy contaminates it with the past, which is why liberated people do not bother with fortunetelling or astrology, and why the happy traveler wanders and does not let himself be the slave of maps, guidebooks, and schedules, using them but not being used by them.

Obviously, there seems to be a paradox in all that I have said here. On the one hand, you do not and actually cannot do anything: it is all happening, as the stream flows of itself. On the other hand, you yourself are no other than this stream—however much you may feel yourself to be some distinct entity in the stream, occasionally controlling it, though mostly driven helplessly along. But the paradox is resolved when you realize that it would be impossible to experience the subjective and voluntary aspect of experience without the contrast of the objective and involuntary. Like all "pairs of opposites" these are two poles of a single process, and our mistake is to identify the reality of self with one only—with the voluntary. Surely it is easy to see that all voluntary action is based on processes that are not voluntary at all, on the circulation of blood and the operation of neural circuits. Nevertheless, if "self" actually comprises both poles, the voluntary and the involuntary are equally your karma, or "action."

Although this provides no specific directions as to how one should act, it changes the mood and feel of action, influencing it somewhat as a change in the tone of voice can

22

alter the effect of one and the same set of words—say from a peremptory command to a polite request. This is the same kind of analogy for what I am trying to describe as that of recovering one's balance in dancing or judo, for the voluntary and the involuntary aspects of experience are like the right and left legs, forming a triangle whose apex is close to the navel and which is the "moving center" of the body. This is why yoga is sometimes said to be contemplation of the navel—a figure of speech for shifting one's center of gravity to a point which transcends the dualism of ego and nonego, since the one cannot exist without the other.

There are many words here, and it is all put more succinctly and clearly by a Zen master who was asked, "How does one enter the Tao?" He answered, "Do you hear the sound of the stream?" . . . "Why, yes." . . . "There is the way to enter."

July 10, 1970

The Chinese characters which I have written on this page are the opening words of the Old Boy's Book of *The Way and Its Power,* otherwise known as Lao-tzu's *Tao Te Ching.* I do not write Chinese very well; an Oriental person looking at my writing knows at once that it was done by a Westerner. Still, they sometimes say that my brushwork is pretty good (for a Westerner), and the young Japanese who are now using ball-point pens instead of brushes say I do it extraordinarily well. But they are a very polite people, and though I have played with the writing brush for many years I am well aware that my technique is nowhere near that of the great masters.

Nevertheless, I have always been in love with Chinese writing. Each character, or ideogram, is an abstract picture of some feature of the process of nature—that is, of the Tao, the Way or Course of the universe. When translated very literally into English, Chinese reads like a telegram. *"Tao* can *tao* not eternal *Tao,"* or "Way can speak-about not eternal Way." In contrast with English, and particularly German or

Flowing with the Tao

25

Japanese, Chinese is the fastest and shortest way of saying things, both in speech and writing. If, as seems possible, Mao-tse Tung's people shift to an alphabetic form of writing, they will be at a great disadvantage, for, as their own proverb says, "One picture is worth a thousand words."

The very mechanics of writing Chinese is an aesthetic delight. It requires a pointed brush with a bamboo handle, the hairs of the brush being lightly impregnated with glue, and brushes come in a delicious variety of sizes and designs —from tiny twigs for writing characters like the footprints of spiders to immense three-inch-wide swabbers for making posters. The ink comes in hard flattened sticks made, essentially, of carbon, glue and perfume, and is embossed with dragons in the clouds or bamboos by the water, or with its brand name in gold characters. A fine old stick of Chinese or Korean ink may fetch as much as $500 on the Japanese market, and I am speaking of a small black object never much more than 6″ x 2″ x 1″. Why? Because of the aesthetic and meditative pleasure of rubbing a fine ink into liquid form upon an ink-stone, which is usually a black rectangular block with rounded corners like a small swimming pool, with a short deep end and a long shallow end. Water is poured upon the stone, and the ink-stick is then rubbed gently and lovingly upon the shallow end until the mixture has just the right viscosity and color, for, under reflected light, the black pigment has to look blue, and the ink-stick has to slide through the water with a certain amiable greasiness. The rubbing takes at least fifteen minutes, and, with the perfume of sandalwood or aloeswood, an artist or calligrapher gets himself in the proper frame of mind to begin his work. Rubbing ink is a form of *za-zen*, or Zen Buddhist meditation in which verbal and conceptual thinking is temporarily suspended. Inferior artists make their apprentices rub the ink. Truly vulgar and depraved artists use bottled ink.

There is a street in Kyoto named Tera-machi (i.e., Temple Street) where, from very small shops, one may buy implements for the tea ceremony, ancient pottery, rosaries, mushrooms, second-hand books, and the most excellent tea in the world. There is also a British-style pub. But the largest shop on the street sells writing brushes, ink, fine paper, and incense. It is one of my paradises, and whenever I get to Kyoto I go there immediately to buy aloeswood (which has, as Dr. Suzuki told me, the essential smell of Buddhism), ink and writing brushes. I just can't resist them. Last time I found a small stick of vermilion ink covered with gold leaf. It should be rubbed on a window sill, early in the morning, using a drop of dew for the water.

It is said to be "difficult" to master the art of Chinese writing, but this means only that the art must grow on you over many years. We use the word "difficult" for tasks which require extreme force or effort, and over which we must perspire, grunt, and groan. But the difficulty of writing Chinese with the brush is to make the brush write by itself, and the Taoists call this the art of *wu-wei*—which may be translated variously as "easy does it," "roll with the punch," "go with the stream," "don't force it," or, more literally, "not pushing." I suppose the Taoist way of life is the polar opposite of Billy Graham's muscular Christianity. *Wu-wei* is the understanding that energy is gravity, and thus that brush writing, or dancing, or judo, or sailing, or pottery, or even sculpture is following patterns in the flow of liquid. Lao-tzu was perhaps the contemporary of that marvelous and neglected Greek philosopher Heraclitus, and both taught exactly the same principles. *Panta rhei*—everything flows, and therefore the understanding of water is the understanding of life. Fire is water falling upwards.

Thus another advantage of Chinese is that, although brief in form, it can say so many things at once. There must be at least eighty English translations of Lao-tzu's book. All differ, and most are to some extent correct. Let us compare differing versions of these six first words:

> The Way that can be described is not the eternal Way.
> The Course that can be discoursed is not the eternal Course.
> The Way that can be weighed is not the regular Way.
> The Flow that can be followed is not the real Flow.
> Energy which is energetic is not true energy.
> Force forced isn't force.

The fourth and fifth characters appear, surprisingly, on planes and trains in the Far East followed by a character which is simply a square, signifying "mouth" or "door." The three put together mean "Emergency exit." Thus:

> The Go that can be gone is an emergency Go.

Most scholars translate the second use of the ideogram *tao* as "to speak about," although Duyvendak has argued that this is a late meaning of the word. But in my own feeling this kind of laconic and aphoristic Chinese is best translated by giving, in parallel, many of the different ways in which it may be understood: for it means all of them. Linear languages like English, German, and Sanskrit have to stretch out Chinese indefinitely. It has thus more or less come to the point where we have simply adopted the word *tao* into English (like karma and curry) and those who call it "tay-o" should realize that in Peking it is called "dow," in Canton "toe," and in Tokyo "daw," and of course Tokyo itself is something like "Tawkyaw."

Tao (which we shall therefore no longer print in different type as a foreign word) signifies the energy of the universe as a way, current, course, or flow which is at once intelligence and spontaneous, but not personal like a Western god. It would be absurd to worship or pray to the Tao because it's your own true self, the very energy and patterning of your bones, muscles, and nerves. Lao-tzu's first statement about it is that it cannot be defined—for the simple reason that you cannot make what is basically you and basically real an *object* of knowledge. You cannot stand aside from it and examine it as something out there. Although, then, we cannot define it, we must not assume that it is something bleary like the "blind energy" of nineteenth-century scientists. From our own points of view our heads themselves are blind spots, but were it otherwise we should be looking only at neurons and dendrites and would never see mountains and trees. (But, of course, when neurons and dendrites are *seen from the inside* they become mountains and trees.)

Yet although Tao cannot be examined and pinned down, it has a characteristic atmosphere which may be sensed in the life-styles of various Far Eastern poets, artists, and sages, and which is indicated by the term *feng-liu* in Chinese and *furyu* in Japanese, and which means something like flowing with or following with the wind. It is also translated as elegance, which is not quite right, because in English an elegant person is refined and fussy, and perpetrates an atmosphere of haughty disdain—whereas the Chinese poet is sometimes amiably drunken, wandering aimlessly in the mountains, and laughing at falling leaves.

One gathers that this sort of person is no longer allowed in China. But he is typified by Pu-tai, the fat, laughing tramp-buddha who carries a gnarled staff and a huge bag of interesting rubbish which he gives away to children.

Poets like Su Tungp'o and Tu Fu were a little more on the side of elegance as we think of it, for they relished drinking fine tea on lazy afternoons, tea made with the best of clear waters from springs and wells, boiled over carefully chosen wood, and served in porcelain or in ceramic bowls with a glaze like jade. On the other hand, a young American Buddhist sought out an extremely holy and magical hermit in the mountains of Japan and, after finding him with extreme difficulty, was served hot water without tea. He had the sense to appreciate the high compliment which he had been offered. Frederic Spiegelberg, philosopher and Orientalist, visited a Taoist hermit like Pu-tai on an island near Hong Kong. When he was introduced as an American university professor traveling under a Rockefeller grant to find out whether Asian spirituality was still vital, the hermit began to chuckle very gently, and this gradually developed into uproarious laughter at which his whole glutaneous mass shook like jelly. That was the end of the interview.

A more ancient Taoist sage, whose name I forget, was approached by a Chinese emperor to be an adviser to the government. He declined the offer with extreme courtesy, but when the emissary had departed he washed out his ears —and also those of the donkey on which he customarily rode. There was also a Chinese Zen priest famed as a great painter, but who, unlike other priests, grew his hair long. After getting sufficiently drunk, he would dip his hair into a bowl of ink and then slosh it over a scroll of paper. The next day he would give himself a Rorschach test on the splosh and see in it images of mountains, rivers, and forests which needed only a few touches of the brush to bring them out for all to see. When I was invited to the tea ceremony by the artist and printmaker Saburo Hasegawa he pointed out the subtle beauty of cigarette ash on a tile made by J. B. Blunk, which we were using for an ashtray.

These are vignettes to give some suggestion of the atmosphere of flowing with the Tao. The principle of the thing is also recognized by our own surf riders, some of whom know very well that their sport is a form of yoga or Taoist meditation in which the whole art is to generate immense energy from going with your environment, from the principle of *wu-wei*, or following the gravity of water and so making yourself one with it. For, as Lao-tzu himself said, "Gravity is the root of lightness."

January 6, 1990

It wasn't until thirty years ago, in the 1960s, that there began to be any widespread realization that ecstasy is a legitimate human need—as essential for mental and physical health as proper nutrition, vitamins, rest, and recreation. Though the idea had been foreshadowed by Freud and stressed by Wilhelm Reich, there had never been anything particularly ecstatic about psychoanalysts, or their patients. They seemed, on the whole, emotionally catharticized and drearily mature. Ecstasy, in the form of mystical experience, had also been the objective of a growing minority that, since the beginning of the century, had been fascinated with yoga, Tibetan Buddhism, Zen, Vedanta, and other forms of Oriental meditation; and these people were always rather serious and demure.

But in the sixties, everything blew up. Something almost like a mutation broke out among people from fifteen to twenty-five, to the utter consternation of the adult world. From San Francisco to Katmandu, there suddenly appeared multitudes of hippies with hair, beards, and costumes that disquietingly reminded their

The Future o
Ecstasy

elders of Jesus Christ, the prophets, and the apostles—who were all at a safe historical distance. At the peak of our technological affluence, these young people renounced the cherished values of Western civilization—the values of property and status. Richness of experience, they maintained, was far more important than things and money, in pursuit of which their parents were miserably and dutifully trapped in squirrel cages.

Scandalously, hippies did not adopt the ascetic and celibate ways of traditional holy men. They took drugs, held sexual orgies and substituted free-loving communities for the hallowed family circle. Those who hoped that all this was just an adolescent quest for kicks that would soon fade away were increasingly alarmed, for it appeared to be in lively earnest. The hippies moved on from marijuana and LSD to Hindu chants and yoga, hardly aware that mysticism, in the form of realizing that one's true self is the Godhead, is something Western society would not tolerate. After all, look what happened to Jesus. Mysticism, or democracy in the kingdom of God, seemed arrant subversion and blasphemy to people whose official image of God had always been monarchical—the cosmic counterpart of the Pharaohs and Cyruses of the ancient world. Mysticism was therefore persecuted alike by church and state, and the taboo still continued—with assistance from the psychiatric inquisition. Admittedly, the hippies were credulous, undiscriminating, and immoderate in their spiritual explorations. But if the approach was fumbling, the goal was clear. I have before me a faded copy of the summer 1969 bulletin of what was then California's revolutionary Midpeninsula Free University (now the world-respected Castalia University of Menlo Park), which bluntly affirms that "The natural state of man is ecstatic wonder; we should not settle for less."

Looking back from 1990, all this is very understandable, however inept. The flower-children knew what their parents hardly dared contemplate: that they had no future. At any moment, they might suffer instant cremation by the H-bomb or the slower and grislier dooms of chemical and biological warfare. The history of man's behavior warned them that armaments which exist are almost invariably used and may even go off by themselves. By the end of 1970, their protests against the power structure of the West (which from their standpoint included Russia), combined with the Black-Power movement, had so infuriated the military-industrial-police-labor-union-Mafia complex known as the establishment that the United States was close to civil war.

Happily, it was just then that the leading scientists, philosophers, and responsible statesmen of the world abruptly called factionists and politicians to their senses. They solemnly proclaimed an ecological crisis and put it so bluntly that the world almost went into panic. Ideological, national, and racial disputes were children's tiffs in comparison with the many-headed menace of overpopulation, totally inadequate food production, shortage of water, erosion of soil, pollution of air and water, deforestation, poisoned food, and utter chemical imbalance of nature. By 1974, no one could refuse to see that all extravagant military and space projects must forthwith be canceled and every energy diverted to feeding and cleansing the world. Had this not happened, I could not be writing to you. Civilization would not have endured beyond 1980 and certainly would not have taken its present direction. For we have gone a long

35

way in persuading people that "the natural state of man is ecstatic wonder."

Because ecstasy was rare, crude, and brief in your day, I should perhaps try to define it. Ecstasy is the sensation of surrendering to vibrations, and sometimes to insights, that take you out of your so-called self. By and large, "self" as a direct sensation is nothing more than chronic neuromuscular tension—a habitual resistance to the pulsing of life; which may explain why nonecstatic people are correctly described as uptight. They are what Freud called anal-retentive types and commonly suffer from impotence and frigidity, being afraid to let themselves go to the spontaneous rhythms of nature. They conceive man as something apart from and even *against* nature, and civilization as an architecture of resistance to spontaneity. It was, of course, this attitude, aided by a powerful technology, that brought about the ecological crisis of the early seventies and, having seen the mistake, we now cultivate ecstasy as we once cultivated literacy or morality.

Do not suppose, however, that we are merely a society of lotus-eaters, lolling on divans and cuddling lovely women. Ecstasy is something higher, or further out, than ordinary pleasure, and few hippies realized that its achievement requires a particular discipline and skill that is comparable to the art of sailing. We do not resist the vibrations, pulses, and rhythms of nature, just as the yachtsman does not resist the wind. But he knows how to manage his sails and, therefore, can use the wind to go wherever he wishes. The art of life, as we see it, is navigation.

Ecstasy is beyond pleasure. Ordinarily, one thinks of the rainbow spectrum of light as a band having red at one end and violet at the other, thus not seeing that violet is the mixture of red and blue. The spectrum could therefore be displayed as a ring of concentric circles instead of a band, but its eye-striking central circle would be where pale, bright yellow comes nearest to white light. This would represent ecstasy. But it can be approached in two ways, starting from violet: through the blues and greens of pleasure or the reds and oranges of pain. This explains why ecstasy can be achieved in battle, by ascetic self-torture, and through the many variations of sadomasochistic sexuality. This we call the left-hand, or negative, approach. The right-hand, or positive, approach is through activities that are loving and life-affirming. Since both approaches reach the same point, it must be noted that ecstasy is always a pleasure/pain experience, as when one weeps for joy or as when there is a certain hurt in intense sexual orgasm.

Pure ecstasy cannot, therefore, be long endured, for, as the Bible says, "No man can see God and live." But frequent plunges into ecstasy transform one's normal consciousness. The everyday world becomes luminous and transparent. The chronic neuromuscular tension against the world disappears, and thus one loses the sensation of carrying one's body around like a load. You feel light, almost weightless, realizing that you are one with a planet that is just falling at ease through space. It's something like the happy, released, energetic feeling one gets after a splendid experience of love-making in the middle of the day.

Continuing the story, you will remember that even as early as 1968, the hippie style of life was, in a superficial form, becoming fashionable in society at large. Beards and longish hair were increasingly noted upon stockbrokers, doctors, professors, and advertising men. Men and women alike began to sport sensuous and psychedelic fabrics and free-form new styles were observed in the highest levels of society. Less publicized was the fact that in these same circles, there was a great deal of experimentation with marijuana and LSD, and a surprising number of successful businessmen became dropouts, fed up with the strain and the dubious rewards of maintaining the uptight posture.

At the same time, various aspects of hippie life and the vaguer, more generalized revolution of youth against the uptight culture began to interest a new generation of film makers and dramatists—young men and women who had already acquired mastery of the techniques of camera and stage and, therefore, brought imaginative discipline into the quest for ecstasy. Fully realizing that their ever-growing market was a population under thirty, they gave a rich and precise articulation to the ambiguous aspirations of the young. They began to replace the old-fashioned, leering style of bawdy film with elegant masterpieces of erotic art. Studying all the new disciplines of sensitivity training and encounter groups (which, by the beginning of 1969, had spread from California and New York to some forty centers all over the United States and Canada), they distinguished truly spontaneous behavior from merely forced imitation of how people might be expected to behave when relieved of all inhibitions.

This point needs some expansion. The encounter group, as it evolved in your time, was a situation in which the participants were encouraged to express their genuine feelings about themselves and one another, barring only physical violence. A variation was the encounter marathon, in which the group stayed together for forty-eight hours, sometimes in the nude to encourage the act of total exposure of oneself to others. But in early experiments, it was soon realized that certain people would fake openness and naturalness, often affecting hostility as the sure sign of being genuine. The problem was that, because very few people really knew how they felt naturally, they would act out their preconceptions of natural and unrestricted behavior, and act merely crudely and lewdly. The encounter group was therefore augmented by sensitivity training, which is the art of abandoning all conceptions of how one *should* feel in order to discover how one actually *does* feel —to get down to pure experience, free from all prejudices and preconceptions of what it is "supposed" to be. The focus is simply on what is now. This is, of course, extremely disconcerting to the habitual role player whose social intercourse is restricted to a finite repertoire of well-rehearsed acts.

The new generation of film makers and dramatists took the experiences of sensitivity training and encounter out onto screen and stage, broke down the barrier of the proscenium arch, made the theater less and less a spectacle and more and more a participatory experience. In film, they produced highly sophisticated versions of the primitive light shows of the sixties, so that audiences became totally immersed in pulsations of sound, light, and pattern. In the early eighties, they used geodesic domes to cover the audience with the screen and get them to dancing with and in paradisiacal films that surrounded the spectator with patterns of iridescent bubbles, animations of Persian miniatures and arabesques, vast enlargements of diatoms and Radiolaria, interior views of intricately cut jewels with landscapes beyond, tapestries of ferns, flowers and foliage, gigantic butterfly wings, Tibetan mandalas, visions of the world as seen by flies, and fantasies of their own which, though anything but vague in form or wishy-washy in color, escaped all possible identification. Such involving presentations were hypnotic and irresistible; even the solidest squares became like those Ukrainian peasants of the ninth century who, on visiting the cathedral of St. Sophia in Byzantium, thought they had arrived in heaven.

The new theater, above all, had everyone rocking with laughter at the attitudes and postures of the uptight world —so much so that, quite outside the theater, it became totally impossible to preach, orate, moralize, or platitudinize before any young audience. One was met with derision or, even more unsettling, with smiling eyes that said. "You've *got* to be putting us on." These developments of screen and stage had much to do with a subsequent advance in psychotherapy; it became the real foundation of an art-science of ecstasy which—not that I like the word—we now call Ecstatics.

Early in 1974, two psychiatrists—Roseman of Los Angeles and Kotowari of Tokyo, then working at UCLA— came up with what we now know as Vibration Training. Like most honest psychiatrists, they felt that their techniques were only scratching the surface and that they were burdened with obsolete maps, assumptions, and procedures based largely on the scientific world-view of the late nineteenth century, which looked at the mind in terms of Newtonian mechanics. Roseman and Kotowari reasoned that the foundation of all experience is a complex of interwoven vibrations of many wave-lengths, dimensions, and qualities. As white light manifests the seven-hued spectrum, so the total spectrum of vibrations has behind it the mysterious E (which $= MC^2$). In their view, a child emerging into the world is the vibration spectrum becoming aware of

40

itself in a particular and partial way, since human senses. are by no means responsive to all known vibrations. (We do not see infrared or gamma rays.) To the baby, these vibrations make neither sense nor nonsense. They are simply what is there. He has no problem about giggling at some or crying at others, since no one has yet taught him which vibrations are good and which are bad. He just goes along uncritically with the whole buzz, without the slightest notion that it is one thing and he another.

But as time goes on, his mother and father, brothers, and sisters teach him how to make sense of the show. By gestures, attitudes and words, they point out what is baby and what is kitty. When he throws up or soils his diapers, they say, "Ugh!" When he sucks on his bottle or swallows Pablum, they say, "Good baby!" They show delight if he smiles, annoyance if he cries and anxiety if he runs a fever or bleeds from a cut. In due course, he has learned all the rudiments of *their* interpretation of what the vibrations are doing and has taken note of their extreme resistance to interpreting them in any other way. Thus, when he asks the name for what is, to him, a clearly shaped area of dry space in a puddle of milk on the table, they say, "Oh, that's nothing." They are very insistent upon what is worth noticing and what isn't, upon wiggles allowed and wiggles forbidden, upon good smells and bad smells (most are bad). The baby has no basis for arguing with this interpretation of the vibrations, and as he grows up, he becomes as fixated on the system of interpretation as his instructors.

But have they given him the correct, or the only possible, interpretation of the system? After all, they got it from their parents, and so on down the line, and who has seriously bothered to check it? We might ask such basic questions as whether the past or the future *really* exists, whether it's really all that important to go on living, whether voluntary and involuntary behavior are genuinely different (what about breathing?) or whether male and female behavior, in gesture and speech, are necessarily distinct in the ways that we suppose. To what extent is the real world simply our own projection upon the vibrations? You have lain in bed looking at some chintz drapes adorned with dauby roses and, all at once, a face appears in the design. As you go on looking, the area surrounding the face begins, if you don't force the process, to form a logical pattern; and the longer you look, the more the whole scene becomes as clear as a photograph. Could we, then, through all our senses, be making some collective projection upon the vibrations, passing it on to our children as the sober truth?

Roseman and Kotowari did not carry their ideas quite that far. Their point was simply that our conceptions of the world are much too rigid and our neuromuscular responses to the vibrations extremely inelastic; that, in other words, we are exhausting and frustrating ourselves with unnecessary defensiveness. They constructed an electronic laboratory where vibrations of all kinds could be simulated, then began to expose themselves and some selected volunteers to various forms of low-energy vibration that would ordinarily be annoying. They tried tickling sensations on various sensitive areas of the skin, the rocking motion of a ship in rough weather, slowly dripping water on the forehead, sounds of fingernails scratching on a blackboard and of squeaky wheels, discordant combinations of musical tones, irritating and incomprehensible melodies, toilet noises, rasping voices with terrible accents, voices that were unctuously insincere, going on to groans, weeping, screams, and maniacal laughter, and finally, all kinds of electronically produced shudders, needles and pins, and nameless sounds. At the beginning of each session, the subject was put into a mild hypnotic state with the one suggestion that he simply give in to whatever vibration is aroused, letting his organism respond freely in whatever way seemed natural. If, for example, a stimulus made him feel like squirming, he was encouraged to squirm as much as he liked and really get with it.

As might be expected, people began to acquire a taste for these formerly taboo vibrations and their new uninhibited and often convulsive responses began to take on an erotic and sometimes ecstatic quality. The doctors supplemented sonic and tactile vibrations with video: strobe lights, vivid color movies of falling through space, of revolting messes accompanied by appropriate smells, of explosions, approaching tornadoes, monstrous spiders, hideous human faces, and of people running through endless crystalline corridors as if totally lost in the mazes of the brain. They then tried low degrees of electronically induced pain, following Grantly Dick-Reid's discovery that labor pains could be reinterpreted as orgiastic tensions, and found that, with a little practice, subjects could tolerate relatively intense degrees of this stimulus—even though writhing and screaming quite unashamedly, yet without giving the doctor any signal to stop.

The researchers also worked with a twenty-four-speaker, 360-degree sound system that surrounded the subject with stereo music of the strongest emotional impact played from twenty-four-track tapes. They had mechanisms for atomizing all kinds of perfume, incense, natural flower scents, and the beneficent aromas of gardens, fields, and forests. They used exquisite and innocently performed erotic movies, filmed kaleidoscopic patterns of jewels and of iridescent whorls of weaving smoke, and mock-ups of unbelievably vast temples and palaces rich with fretted screens and polychrome sculpture. The subject would be visually, aurally, olfactorily, and kinesthetically led through their enormous courtyards, gardens, galleries, naves, and sanctuaries to the accompaniment of angelic choirs, sonorous trumpets, double-bass-throated bells and gongs, and unearthly chants and hymns, until the journey reached its climax in a holy of holies where he might be confronted with a remarkably beautiful goddess or a colossal aureole of rich and brilliant light into which he would be finally absorbed—to find himself soaring bodilessly in clear-blue sky, like a seagull. Sometimes they accompanied this climax with electrical stimulation of the pleasure centers of the brain.

It should be noted that, through all this, the gadgetry was, as far as possible, installed in a separate room, away from the subject, who lay in a spacious neutral chamber with walls that could be decorated in any way desired by light projection. Those who volunteered for a course of this treatment discovered that their responses to the ordinary, everyday vibration system were radically changed. Almost all uptightness had disappeared, for they had learned how to reinterpret and actually dig the vibratory sensations hitherto called anxiety, fear, grief, depression, shame, guilt, and a considerable degree of what they had known as pain.

It was as if the science of electronics had thus far just been waiting for something important to do. From every continent, electronic buffs got in touch with Roseman and Kotowari with suggestions and requests for information, and it was only a few months before similar laboratories were set up in cities all over the world. Shortly afterward, such corporations as Bell Telephone and Varian Associates began to design miniaturized versions of the equipment, which could be mass-produced, so that by 1979 it had become the major technique for psychotherapy, and a large research center for the two doctors was established at Castalia University.

The general effect was that uptightness came to be recognized as a sickness, like alcoholism or paranoia, so that more and more people began to be increasingly comfortable in a world where truth and reality were far less rigidly defined. They stopped looking for rocks on which to stand and foundations for building their lives, dropping all such metaphors of fortification and stony solidity. They realized that the world, the vibration system, is more airy and liquid than solid and they reacted to it as swimmers, sailors, and airmen rather than as landlubbers. They found security in letting go rather than in holding on and, in so doing, developed an attitude toward life that might be called psychophysical judo. Nearly twenty-five centuries ago, the Chinese sages Lao-tzu and Chuang-tzu had called it *wu-wei*, which is perhaps best translated as "action without forcing." It is sailing in the stream of the Tao, or course of nature, and navigating the currents of *li* (organic pattern)—a word that originally signified the natural markings in jade or the grain in wood.

As this attitude spread and prevailed in the wake of Vibration Training, people became more and more indulgent about eccentricity in life-style, tolerant of racial and religious differences, and adventurous in exploring unusual ways of loving. Present time became more important than future time, on the reasoning that there is no point in making plans for the future if you can't fully enjoy their results when they, in turn, become part of the present. By and large, we stopped rushing and found that with less haste, we had more speed, since rushing sets up a whole multitude of antagonistic vibrations. We got out of uptight clothes—trousers, girdles, neckties, hard shoes, and other contraptions for trussing and binding the body, as if to say, "Now you really exist and will not fall apart." We shifted into every variety of colorful sarong, kimono, sari, caftan, burnous, and poncho and wore them on the streets and for business. We equipped our homes with spacious Japanese bathtubs or saunas, where we all sat and relaxed after the day's work. These tubs were made so that six people could sit with hot water up to their necks; and, of course, one did not wash in the tub itself but took a shower first. Several of my friends in California had them back in the sixties, but now they're everywhere.

Absence of rush gave us a very new and different approach to sexual relations. You must understand that despite the ecological crisis of the seventies, technology gave us an enormous amount of leisure. By 1985, there were no longer nine-to-five jobs. The whole world began to run on Greenwich mean time, and work hours today are staggered throughout each twenty-four-hour period, amounting in all to about ten hours a week—unless, of course, one is an enthusiast for doctoring, engineering, scientific research, or carpentry, in which case he can work as long as he likes. Under these circumstances, we no longer speak of sexual relations as sleeping or going to bed with someone. After all, why wait until you're tired? Furthermore, late-night or early-morning sex in bed tends to restrict the relationship to simple fucking, so that the whole thing is over in from two to twenty minutes. Men in a hurry to prove—what?

We take our time. The man and the woman take turns to manage the occasion, the one acting as servant of the other (although this is no rigid pattern and the arrangement may also be mutual). One begins by serving his beloved a light but exquisite meal, which is usually eaten from a low table surrounded with large floor cushions. It should be explained that today most men know how to cook and that for many years people have been keeping their legs limber by sitting on the floor. For the meal, the couple wear loose and luscious clothes, and often the cooking is done at the table over an electric Permacoal or ordinary charcoal fire. As is now customary (and, I should add, quite legal), a water pipe is brought to the table after the meal for the smoking of marijuana or hashish, since it is now recognized that any alcohol other than light wine or beer is not conducive to sexual ecstasy.

So as not to interfere with conversation during the meal, music is not played until the pipe is brought. Vibration Training has abolished mere background music, and it is now considered extremely bad taste not to listen whenever music is played. The music may be recorded, but sometimes one or two friends, or even the children of the couple, come in at this time with instruments and play for an hour or so while the pipe is smoked; and, after the serving partner clears the table, the couple adjourn to the bath for showers and a half-hour soak in the big tub. The serving partner then gives his or her companion a complete massage on a special pad provided in the bathroom. (Toilet facilities, I should note, are always in a separate room.) While the one who has received the massage takes a short rest, the other lays out a thick, fold-up floor pad by the table, setting beside it a basket of flowers, a box of jewels, and a make-up kit. Sometimes a pair of tall candlesticks is placed at each end of the pad, and incense, in a burner with a long wooden handle, is set on the table.

The other person is then escorted, naked, from the bathroom and seated on the pad, and he or she is then adorned with jewels—usually an elaborate (but nonscratchy) necklace with matching wrist and ankle bracelets. The incense burner is lifted by its handle and used to perfume the hair and, thereafter, make-up is applied decoratively and imaginatively to the eyes, lips, and forehead, and often to other parts of the body. The forehead, for example, is usually adorned with a small "third eye" design such as is used among Hindu dancers. Flowers are then set in the hair and, perhaps, hung around the neck in the form of a *lei*. The serving partner usually puts on his or her own adornments immediately after the massage, during the rest.

Both are now seated on the pad, facing each other. One of the benefits of Vibration Training is that it allows almost everyone to have a good singing voice, for the blocks against producing a clear tone have been removed. Therefore, it is now quite usual for lovers to sing to each other, with a hummed chant or with articulate words, sometimes using a guitar or a lute. It is thus that, before bodily contact begins, they caress each other with their eyes while singing. Some people prefer, at this time, to play such games as checkers, dominoes or ten-second chess, the winner having the privilege of proposing any form of sex-play desired. From this point on, almost anything goes, though the mood established by the preparations is often conducive to a long, slow form of sexual intercourse wherein the couple remain joined for an hour or more with very little motion, keeping the preorgasmic tension as high as possible without aiming at the release of climax. I realize that, back in the seventies, most men would consider this ritual affected and ridiculous and term the whole business a good honest fuck spoiled. Looking back, it is amazing to realize how unconscious we were of our barbarity, our atrocious manners, our slipshod cooking, our uncomfortable clothes, and our absurdly grace-less and limited sex acts.

Something more should be said about our use of psyche-delics. Today these substances are given the same kind of respect that has always been accorded to the very finest French wines. Anyone, for example, who smokes them throughout the day is regarded as a crude guzzler incap-able of appreciating their benefits. They are not used at ordinary parties amid chitchat and gossip, but only under circumstances in which the fullest attention may be given to the changes in consciousness that they confer. Thus, they are taken more as religious sacraments than as kicks, though today our religious attitudes are not pious or sanctimonious, since only very ignorant people now think of God as the cosmic stuffed shirt in whose presence no laughter is allowed.

I well remember the first great hemp shop that was opened in San Francisco around 1976. It was essentially a long wooden bar with stools for the customers. On the bar itself were a few large crocks containing the basic and cheaper forms of the weed—Panama Red, Acapulco Gold, Indian Ganja, and Domestic Green. But against the wall behind the bar stood a long cabinet furnished with hundreds of small drawers that a local guitar maker had decorated

49

with intricate ivory inlays in the Italian style. Each drawer carried a label indicating the precise field and year of the product, so that one could purchase all the different varieties from Mexico, Lebanon, Morocco, Egypt, India, and Vietnam, as well as the carefully tended plants of devout cannabinologists here at home. Business was conducted with leisure and courtesy, and the salesmen offered small samples for testing at the bar, along with sensitive and expert discussion of their special effects. I might add that the stronger psychedelics, such as LSD, were coming to be used only rarely—for psychotherapy, for retreats in religious institutions, and in our special hospitals for the dying.

These latter became common after about 1978, when some of the students of Roseman and Kotowari realized that the sensation of dying could be reinterpreted ecstatically as total self-release. As a result, death became an occasion for congratulations and rejoicing. After all, "You only die once" (as the slogan went), and if death is as proper and natural as birth, it is absurd not to make the most of it. Even today, the science of geriatrics is far from conferring physical immortality, though it is increasingly common for people to pass their 100th or even 150th birthdays. Our hospitals for the dying are the work of our most imaginative architects and are set about with orchards and flower gardens, fountains and spas, and we have utterly forsaken the grisly and hollow rituals of mid-century morticians. Even the young have been taught to contemplate without creeps and shudders the prospect of their annihilation, by means of exposure—in the course of Vibration Training—to intense light and sound, followed by total darkness and silence.

And we now have something *completely* new. You will

remember that, in 1969, Dr. Joseph Weber of the University of Maryland discovered and measured gravity waves. This led, in 1982, to a method for polarizing the force of gravity that has revolutionized transportation, abolished smog, and so redistributed population that densely crowded cities no longer exist. Three physicists—Conrad, Schermann, and Grodzinski—found a way of polarizing a material similar to lead so as to give it a negative weight in proportion to its positive, or normal, weight. This material can be attached to the back of a strong, wide belt, carrying also the requisite electronic equipment, plus directional and volume controls, thus enabling the wearer to float off the ground or shoot high into the air. At low volume, one can take enormous strides, a mile long and fifty feet high at the peak, or float gently through valleys and over the tops of trees without rush or noise. At high volume and dressed in a space suit, one can soar into outer space or travel easily at three hundred miles an hour at four thousand feet. Needless to say, every such outfit is equipped with a radar device that brings one to a hovering halt the moment there is any danger of collision. Much larger units of the leadlike material are attached to freight and passenger aircraft, and the silent ease of vertical ascent and descent has freed us from all the hassle and inconvenience of the old airports.

But we are not in a hurry. As a result, negative gravitation has given us everything for which we envied the birds, and it is much used for the sport of lolling about in the air, for skydiving and dancing, for "sitting" on clouds, and for reaching homes now built on otherwise inaccessible mountaintops and in secluded valleys. You will remember the reports of the ecstasy of weightlessness given long ago by spacemen, skydivers, and skindivers. Now this is available to everyone, and we literally float about our business. As Toynbee foresaw, civilization has become etherealized; grass grows on the highways, and earth has been relieved of all its concrete belts and patches.

Of course, the main problem of the ecstatic life is comparable to fatigue in metals: it is impossible to remain at a peak of ecstasy for a long time, even when the types of ecstasy are frequently varied. Furthermore, consciousness tends to repress or ignore a perpetual stimulus—such as the sea-level pressure of air on the skin. This has given us a new respect for mild asceticism. Since the ecological crisis, enormous numbers of people have taken to gardening, and cultivate fruits and vegetables on every scrap of arable land, using large Fuller domes as hothouses in winter, which itself is much milder than it used to be, thanks to worldwide climate control. Millions are therefore up by six in the morning (your time), digging, hoeing, weeding and pruning. At the same time, we eat much less in bulk and no longer expect disgustingly overloaded plates in restaurants. Not only is our food more nutritive but we also find our stamina and muscle tone much better for lack of stuffing ourselves. Despite the advantages of negative gravitation, we walk and hike almost religiously, for with our wealth of gardens, the landscape is worth seeing and the unpaved ground is easy on the feet. Ample time and absence of rush likewise encourage patient and highly skilled work in all types of art and craft. You would, I suppose, call us fanatical hobbyists—a world of experts in whatever one loves to do, from athletics to zoology.

We are much aware of *little* ecstasies—the sensation of carving wood with a really sharp chisel, timeless absorption in making carpets as glowing as the finest Orientals, laying down and polishing parquet floors in various natural colors of wood, bottling dried herbs from the garden, unraveling tangled string, listening to wind bells made of sonor (a new and marvelously resonant metal), selecting and arranging painted tiles for a chessboard, expertly boning a fish, roasting chestnuts over charcoal in the evening, combing a woman's hair, or washing and massaging a friend's feet. As soon as we freed ourselves from the mirage of hurrying time —which was nothing more than the projection of our own impatience—we were alive again, as in childhood, to the miracles and ecstasies of ordinary life. You would be astounded at the beauty of our homes, our furniture, our clothes, and even our pots and pans, for we have the time to make most of these things ourselves, and the sense of reality to see that they—rather than money—constitute genuine wealth.

We also cultivate something oddly known as the ecstasy of ordinary consciousness—related, it would seem, to the Zen principle that "Your usual consciousness is Buddha," meaning here the basic reality of life. We have become accustomed to living simultaneously on several levels of reality, some of which appear to be in mutual contradiction —as your physicists could regard the nucleus as both particle and wave. In your time, the overwhelmingly orthodox view of the world was objective; you took things to be just as scientists described them, and we still give due weight to this point of view. Taken by itself, however, it degrades man to a mere object: it defines him as he is seen from outside and so screens out his own inside vision of things. Therefore we also take into account the subjective, naive, and childlike way of seeing life and give it at least equal status. It was, I think, first shown by a British architect,

Douglas Harding, writing in the early sixties, that from this point of view, one has no head. The only directly perceptual content of the head, he wrote, especially through the eyes and ears—which are directed outward from the head—is everything *except* the head. Once this obvious but overlooked fact becomes clear, you no longer regard your head as the center of consciousness; you cease to be a central *thing* upon which experience is banging, scratching, and being recorded. Thus, the center of awareness becomes one with all it perceives. You and the world become identical, and this disappearance of oneself is, to say the least, a blissful release.

This way of interpreting reality does not contradict the scientific way any more than the colorlessness of a lens rejects the colors of flowers. On the contrary, it restores a whole dimension of value to life which your passion for objectivity neglected, and, by comparison, your exclusively scientific universe seems a desiccated, rattling, and senseless mechanism. Though it was *self*-centered, in the largest sense, it left out man himself. We have put him back—not as a definable object but as the basic and supreme mystery. And as the Dutch philosopher Aart van der Leeuw once put it, "The mystery of life is not a problem to be solved but a reality to be experienced."

January 1972

As far back as I can remember, I have always been fascinated by the idea of death. I think most children are. "If I should die before I wake . . ." The prospect of going to sleep and *never* waking up is unthinkable but compellingly fascinating. One must agree, then, with Albert Camus that the only really serious philosophical question is whether or not to commit suicide. Because this is not just a matter of going forever into a state of darkness, like being buried alive or going blind. It is not only to have no future, to pass *into* a state of total blankness; it is also to be as if one had never been at all, to have neither present nor past. It would be as if, not only myself, but also the whole universe had never existed. And there would be no one to miss, regret, or object to the loss. No problems at all.

At least, this would be the common-sense of the matter, abandoning all ideas of personal survival as wishful thinking without basis in any reliable evidence. Most intelligent and skeptical people take this to be the way things are, realize that nothingness is

The Reality of Reincarnation

inconceivable, shrug their shoulders, and think no more of it. But I have never been able to be content with letting it go at that. I continue, as one spellbound, to contemplate, to try to imagine the state (or is it the nonstate?) of nothingness.

When I ask myself the seemingly meaningless question what it is *like* to be nothing and never to have been, I think first of the way my own head looks to my eyes. For, going by the sense of sight alone, there is not, right behind my eyes, a dark place, or a hazy place. There is a positive sensation of nothing—which is quite different from saying that there isn't anything, because, after all, I *see* out of this nothingness.

The second idea that comes to mind is that when I am dead I will be (or "it" will be) just as I was before I was born. In both states, after death and before birth, it is as if I—and all else—had never been at all. Most people, again, shrug their shoulders and say, "We come from nothing and we return to nothing—and that's the end of it." But I demur. For it strikes me as utterly amazing that I did in fact come from this nothing. If I came from it once, I see no reason why I could not come from it again; for if, as is indeed the case, I did come from it once, this nothingness is, to say the least, unexplainably frisky.

Now let me put together these two ideas of what nothingness is *like*. I try to go back and back in memory to how it was before I was born, and find a blank. I try to turn about and see what is immediately behind my eyes and also find a blank. But in both cases I have other evidence for knowing that something is there. Before I was born, there were my father and mother, the earth, the sun, moon, and stars, the galaxy, and the whole energy of the universe—

and then space, another seeming blank. All this is blank because I have no memory or sensation of it as it was before I was born.

In the same way I know that behind my eyes is my invisible brain. I do not understand it or remember how I grew it, or how my father and mother grew it, and I have no direct sensation of it. Therefore it is blank. But my *seeing* comes out of it in just the same sort of way that my *being* comes out of my father and mother, and the whole universe behind them, and the space "behind" it. As my unseen brain sees with my eyes, my unremembered past (which is the still continuing world) feels with my body.

So, if I go back to the "nothing" before I was born and out of which I came, I find this very real and active universe. I have also the best evidence for believing that this same universe will be just as real and active after I am dead, for I have seen others die and then others born, and it still goes on.

Now where in all this am I to locate my *self*? Most of us would agree without much argument that the unseen brain is more essentially *me* than the eyes, since a blind person still feels that he exists. But where am I to locate my self when I consider that, just as my brain sees with my eyes, the universe feels with my body? In other words, my body and all bodies come forth from this whirl of energy as leaves come from trees and fish from the ocean and, most remarkably, stars from space.

If, then, I identify my self exclusively with my body, I separate it from the whirl of energy which "grew" me and, for that matter, is still growing me with its light, heat, air, and water. Yet if I identify my self with the whole whirl (which would be perfectly reasonable) people would say,

"Who the hell do you think you are? You don't run this universe." To which I reply, "Who the hell do you think *you* are? You don't know how your brain works. You haven't the faintest idea how you shaped your skeleton." It is, then, just as reasonable to say that my self is the whole whirl as to say that it is just this particular body, for I don't consciously manage either. I don't warm up the galaxy. I don't design my nervous system. It happens, and I happen. My self does not manage itself as if it were something outside itself like an automobile or a typewriter. So if I don't manage my self—if only defined as this body—there is no reason why I shouldn't define my self as the whole universe. Considering all, the latter definition is far more reasonable.

Furthermore, it seems obvious that the universe is a system which, by means of living bodies, becomes aware of itself—up to a point. Just as there is a blank behind the eyes, and just as you can't kiss your own lips, the universe cannot know itself completely. If it could, there would be no surprises, and that would spoil the fun. Existence would be like making love to a plastic woman.

With all this in mind, we can take a reasonable approach to the problem of death. By that I mean that we can clarify the problems without recourse to spookery—to divine revelations, to other people's alleged psychic experiences, to spiritual teachers of questionable authority, or to any kind of unverifiable hocus-pocus. Without resorting to anything beyond what we all know; without supposing the existence of anything like an immortal soul, it can, for example, be shown that the ancient and popular idea of reincarnation is completely rational. I will not go so far as to say that I can prove it; but I can come close to that, and with better evidence than is available for many things that are taken as a matter of course.

To explain myself I will have to invent the verb "to I," which, with a convenient pun, has the same kind of sense as "to eye"—and I will spell it that way to avoid clumsy typography. So the universe "eyes" in the same way that a tree "apples" and space "stars." (You can always turn a noun into a verb because every *thing* is also an *event*, a happening. Houses are "housing.")

My body, your body, everybody is the universe eyeing. Presumably to go beyond partiality and prejudice, it eyes with myriads of different bodies and keeps changing them. Variety is the spice of life. And because each body is the universe eyeing, everyone feels that he or she is "I." Obviously, after the death of any one body, other bodies come into being, and in every case they have just the same experience of coming out of nothing as you and I had when we were born. So when the universe stops eyeing with my body, *this* body, it goes on with others, and all these others feel themselves as much "myself" as I do now.

I know, then, that after I die other bodies, other eyeings, will be born. But this is really the same thing as saying that after I die I will again awake as a baby—any baby, but only one—just as I did before but without remembering the previous trip. For anyone who argues that after death there will be nothingness forever is really saying that when he dies the universe will cease to be. But we know that it goes on after people die, and that because *it* does the eyeing it is really more my self than this particular body. If any apple could become fully aware it would say, "I am what the tree is doing." Thus if the universe has eyed me once it can eye me again. For effect I have put the word "me" in that sentence; if you doubt its truth, cross it out, and the sentence will be unquestionably true. And it will mean almost the same thing—because eye = me.

But to believe in reincarnation we must show that there can be some particular connection between two distinct eyeings that do not overlap in time, as do father and son. If I talk about the universe "eyeing" me again, I am supposing that it will again produce another body, another life, so close to mine in style and character that it could be recognized as a return of Alan Watts. "Cold comfort," you may object, "because that will still be someone else, even if your very double." Nevertheless, I can show that there could be just as much connection between that other Alan Watts and myself as there is between myself today and myself tomorrow.

It all depends on what we mean by connection. Look at any magazine photograph with a magnifying glass. Firm and continuous lines will dissolve into disconnected dots. Or go in the other direction. From close by, our galaxy appears to be a dispersal of disconnected stars, but from far off we would see the form of a spiral nebula. There are no "strings" connecting these stars. What connects them is that they form a pattern, in the same way as the dots in the magazine photograph. Patterns are not only configurations in space but also rhythms in time and, as such, are things, forms, and events just as real and solid as anything else that we can experience. Solid steel is a pulsating gyration of electrons and positrons separated by relatively colossal spaces, and physicists cannot quite make up their minds whether they are particles or waves.

Continuous time-patterns are also revealed by fast-motion pictures of growing plants, or by speeding up the projector in a planetarium to such a pace that the planets seem to trace continuous lines across the dome. In the motion picture the plant is seen to be making a definite, formal gesture—like opening one's hand—which is not ordinarily seen. In the planetarium the actual course or orbit of the planets becomes visible. Indeed, whatever we experience as existing, as continuing in time, is not so much persistent stuff as repetitive rhythm or vibration.

Although it would be technically impossible to show a fast-motion picture of the courses of myriads of human lives between, say, 10,000 B.C. and the present, it would not be unreasonable to think that, if it could be done, we would recognize connections of pattern between separate courses. We could see a series of lives running from 10,000 to 9,930, from 8,500 to 8,430, and from 8,300 to 8,240, in which three different individuals were tracing out a coherent pattern of behavior. At that speed they would seem just as much three appearances of one individual as someone you met successively at perhaps seven-year intervals. For the coherent continuity of any one individual is much like a whirlpool in a river; it is "there" day after day, although the water itself never stays put. You could even say that there is no such thing as a whirlpool, but that the river is whirlpooling in the same way that the universe eyes and the plant flowers.

You could argue that no such connections or continuities would exist without someone or something, like an observer or a camera, to record them. But then, to be consistent, you would have to say that the spiral pattern of a galaxy doesn't really exist until it is observed. It would be the same argument to say that there could be no real continuity between one life and another unless it had been "photographed" on one's memory. But this will force you into arguing that a tree in a lonely valley isn't there until someone sees it, and if you insist on following that line of reasoning you will at last be forced to claim that you are God imagining the universe. That might be true, but it isn't the sort of position that scientific and skeptical people want to adopt.

You might also argue that, given an observer, no such connections would be seen. This is utterly unlikely, because even among things so randomly distributed as the heavenly bodies we see galaxies, constellations, and the solar system; we find beauty in clouds and spray, and music in the sound of water. That we do so may have much to do with the structure of our senses and nerves, but they are, in turn, part of the system. It makes sense of itself in the act of eyeing, of sensing.

If you have followed me this far you will have stopped worrying about death. You will have realized that to be or not to be is *not* the question, because you are a repeatable act of eyeing on the part of a system, a universe, that has perfectly well been able to take care of itself for at least 10,000 million years. And considering that, by means of death, it provides itself with a periodic forgettory as well as a memory, and also that it beholds itself in such improbable forms as giraffes and toucans, you may well be assured that it (i.e., you) will never be bored.

I have been trying, then, to show the extreme likelihood of a reincarnation process without resorting to any evidence from the field of parapsychology and psychic research, in which such responsible investigators as Ian Stevenson have studied large numbers of people who claim vivid memories of former lives. (Dr. Stevenson is chairman of the Department of Neurology and Psychiatry at the University of

Virginia School of Medicine and author of *Twenty Cases Suggestive of Reincarnation,* published in 1966 by the American Society for Psychical Research.) To most scientists this evidence is still suspect because, for one thing, the human mind is a fertile field for hallucinations and, for another, there has been no scientifically acceptable and respectable theory to support it. But if Dr. Stevenson can establish, in one case alone, that a person remembers details of a former life which he cannot have discovered by ordinary means (and I think he has established it in more than one case), all we need is an intellectually respectable theory to account for it.

But it should be noted as an amusing aside that what is intellectually respectable is often a matter of academic fashion. When the great Austrian entomologist Von Fritsch proved beyond all doubt that bees use language, an entomologist at the University of California expressed "passionate reluctance" to accept the evidence. Why the emotional reaction? Because in much of the academic and scientific community it is a point of honor, a rubric of ritual, and a requirement of intellectual etiquette that one abstain from saying anything that might remind one's colleagues of religion, mysticism, magic, or the supernatural—or anything to suggest that forms of life other than human are truly intelligent. Up to a point this is a healthy attitude with which I am not arguing, except to remind such academicians of their overly heavy emotional investment in maintaining it. In the meantime I prefer to play the game by their rules.

I have been explaining a theory of connection between bodies or forms that are separate in space, such as electrons and positrons or stars, or distinct in time, such as the individual pulses of a musical tone or of cosmic rays. I have also suggested that still more widely separated events, such as individual life-courses and the appearance and disappearance of stellar systems, can also be considered as pulses in a continuing rhythm or time-pattern. This is akin to the proposal of the British biophysicist Launcelot L. Whyte that the unitary principle of all systems be considered as their form (or pattern). This simple and elegant idea is extremely hard to explain to people who have had it rubbed into their minds that the world operates like a game of billiards wherein solid balls of stuff shove each other around, and must therefore be explained on the basis of Who Pushed Whom? There is nothing in the least unscientific about Whyte's idea because forms can be measured, counted, and described, whereas pure and undifferentiated stuff is utterly inconceivable.

Right here is the main reason why any memory of former lives cannot be explained "scientifically." For scientists— especially engineers, and even some physicists—still have it in the back of their minds (though many of them know better) that all physical processes must be inscribed and transmitted on basic stuff. It seems, then, that to explain remembrance of past lives there would have to be some sort of imperishable stuff or substance to carry the memories, like a photographic film. But that would be just exactly what was meant by the crude sense of the old-fashioned soul or spirit, which neither I nor the scientific community wants to drag in.

If, however, we won't allow ourselves to drag it in to explain memories of former lives, we can't use it to explain memories of last Tuesday. There seems to be no problem about remembering last Tuesday because we have all been tacitly assuming that its events have been imprinted on the stuff of our brains and bodies. Yet there is no such stuff, just as there are no strings connecting the stars of the galaxy or electrons of the atom. Just as the physicists have never been able to detect any spiritual stuff, they have never found any material stuff. They have found measurable shapes, structures, patterns, and pulses—all with lots of space between them—but no undifferentiated goo out of which these forms are "made," like pots from clay. If you ever did find this basic stuff, how would you talk about it? It would entirely elude formal and structural description. All along the whole notion of material stuff has been a superstition as gross as werewolves and banshees. What we really experience as stuff is nothing more than form seen out of focus, for you can't see the detailed structure of kapok or clay until you look at it with a microscope. Then it is no longer fuzzy or gooey stuff; it is crystal clear.

Thus when a scientist like Ian Stevenson finds someone who remembers a former life, what can he do except check out the story in just the same way as he would verify someone's account of what happened last Tuesday? A small boy in Thailand, or Japan, takes us to a village where he has never been, shows us the way around, and introduces us to all his old friends. So he remembers. We don't like to admit it (we say because we can't explain it) but the truth is that while there is some evidence for reincarnation, we have a theory against it. We don't rule out the stars as hallucinations on the theory that light *cannot* pulse across empty space where there is no ether, no stuff to carry its waves. We don't make the initial supposition that all tales are lies or fantasies until it is proved otherwise, or until we know more about the nervous system, or about the relation of mind to brain. But in a cultural situation where reincarnation has been both theologically and scientifically heretical, we are not likely to encourage or listen to little children when they speak of it.

In sum, then, I have tried to show that reincarnation has very strong theoretical probability, without resorting to the paranormal evidence and even without being able to explain the transmission of memories. I have carefully avoided bringing in the moral and retributive arguments, since they have little force, and I do not find a person's fortunes or misfortunes explained by a former life. I find the explanation postponed, as in all attempts to explain the present by the past. But it is basically an intellectual block to find it incredible that you have more than one life. It is just as incredible that we have this one. It is still more incredible to suppose that what has happened once cannot happen again.

February 25, 1971

The Hindu-Buddhist theory of karma is at once simpler and more complex than is generally supposed. Popularly, karma is viewed as an almost mechanical system of retribution whereby evil action bears evil consequences, and good action good consequences, to the doer—in this present life, or in some life to come. Evil action towards another being is, at the same time, his own karma and the result of his own evil action, and also brings evil to the offender. Good action is the karmic merit of the recipient, and brings merit to the doer. Karma is not popularly understood as fate, for at any time one may freely initiate good or evil karma regardless of karma accumulated from the past. Karma is therefore seen as a moral law of cause and effect built into the structure of the universe.

Actually, the word karma means simply "action" or "doing" and does not imply that the universe involves an impersonal system of moral justice which recognizes and weighs human conventions of good and evil. Thus if we say of someone killed in an airplane crash that it was his karma, it means just that the apparent

Implications of Karma

67

accident was his own doing, and the doing of all those involved. Furthermore, Buddhist philosophy does not admit the real existence of any nuclear ego which could cause or be the recipient of karma. The apparent identity of an enduring being by whom deeds are done and to whom they happen is understood as nothing more than a continuing pattern in and of the stream of deeds, as when a stone is tossed into a pool, no body of water, called "a wave," moves outwards from the point of impact. The water moves up and down, perpendicularly, and the horizontal movement of the wave is through the water, but not of it. The horizontally moving ridge of the wave is not the same water at the circumference as it was at the center, as may easily be seen by throwing a dollop of dye into its path—for the dyed water will stay in the same lateral position. Buddhists therefore regard a "self" who goes through life like a passenger in a train as an illusion, as is also the vertical motion of a laterally revolving barber's pole.

My karma is thus the action or behavior of an enduring pattern, like the crest-trough formation of a wave, which is recognized in 1971 as in 1950 as Alan Watts or, better, as Alan Wattsing. But this pattern consists equally of what the pattern is said to do and of what is said to happen to it. Both constitute its behavior or motion, for I could not walk if the sun were not keeping me warm. My physical shape is as much produced by the expansive strength of my bones and muscles as by the pressure of air around and upon them. Or, in other words, the way my pattern works derives as much from heredity as from environment. So too, the pattern of a river comes equally from the gravity of the water and the lay of the land.

What, then, is the point of saying that what happens to

me, involuntarily or accidentally, is my own karma or doing? It is to say, first, that there would be nothing recognizable as me unless there were also something recognizable as not-me, and that we cannot identify what someone does voluntarily unless we can at the same time identify what happens to him involuntarily. We can then go on to say, second, that because the Alan Watts pattern or doing or karma involves both it *is* both. If my karma is both what I do and what happens to me then I am not, as I imagined, just one aspect of the process. I am not just the giving-and-receiving aspect, but also the happening which goes on outside anything usually recognized as me. But we are one-sided in our thinking and attention and, as Gestalt psychology has long pointed out, notice the figure and ignore the background. But the new totality or self, recognized when both the voluntary and the involuntary aspects of one's karma are taken into consideration, goes far beyond anything that can be narrowly and one-sidedly defined as Alan Watts or John Doe. If I cannot be my particular "self" except in relation to the particular "other," or environment, which surrounds me, then we have a situation in which every identifiable pattern in the universe implies all the others. In Mahayana Buddhist philosophy this is called the *dharmadhatu,* the mutual interpenetration and interdependence of all things and events—one in all, and all in one.

The same conclusion is reached from those viewpoints of Hindu philosophy which accord at least some reality to the ego as the *purusha* or *jivatman* which is the witness or knower behind all that I experience. But the point will be expressed in a different way. If I realize that everything which happens to me, i.e., the rest of the universe, is my karma or doing, I will then realize that my particular *jivat-*

man is actually the *atman,* the supra-individual Self, which is identical with Brahman, the Self of the universe. If central "self" and peripheral "other" are, however different explicitly, mutually interdependent, they are implicitly one. What is explicitly dual, or *dvaita,* is implicitly nondual, or *advaita.* Whether the point of departure is Buddhist or Hindu, the conclusion is the same realization of "cosmic consciousness" in which consciousness is not restricted to its fixation on the voluntary, central, and individualized aspect of karma.

So long as this restriction continues we take side with the voluntary aspect and thus try to extend it indefinitely. We own what we do and disown what happens, and go on to expand the area which we can own and control. Technology, as now practiced, is one of the principal means of this expansion, but we are just beginning to see that this extension of the voluntary is also extension of the involuntary, because our behavior is increasingly controlled by the nature and structure of our machinery. Our food, clothing, housing, traveling, and general behavior must increasingly be dictated by mechanical efficiency to the point—already passed—where we cannot live without it. It is even conceivable that machinery is creating an environment in which only machines can live, that it will capture the voluntary aspect of karma and eliminate the biological world by regimentation and asphyxiation. Its operations are not restrained or confused by emotions or tender feelings. But, on the other hand, our very strength is in the possibility of feeling for, or owning, what is other than ourselves—and if machines cannot accomplish this transcendence of self and other they will destroy themselves faster than people have done the same.

70

Overstressing the voluntary aspect of karma is ignore-
ance (*avidya*) of the other, which is in turn that craving
or grasping (*trishna*) of control described by the Buddha
as the root of suffering. His *dharma* or method of life was,
instead, the Middle Way of compassion—that is, of feeling
for both sides, of allowing, respecting, and owning the
apparently random and involuntary aspect of our karma.
This means increasing tolerance for surprising and unsched-
uled events, for life-forms and life-styles other than our
own, and for all things sinuous, slippery, wayward, and
wiggly as distinct from straight, square, boxed, and classified in defiance of the curvaceous forms of the natural
world. Perhaps the music of Handel has made us blind to
the real horror of Isaiah's words—

> The voice of him that crieth in the wilderness, "Prepare
> ye the way of the Lord, make straight in the desert a high-
> way for our God." Every valley shall be exalted, and every
> mountain and hill shall be made low: and the crooked
> shall be made straight, and the rough places plain.

It is happening all over California.

When we fight the environment and disown it, our
methods and weapons become part of it, part of the involuntary and uncontrollable component of karma. This, as in
the tale of the Sorcerer's Apprentice, is the fate of all power
games, not only in the areas of material power but also in
those of psychic and spiritual power. This is why one should
not be misled by the many forms of mental and psychic
discipline which promise greater and greater control over
thought and emotion, and even magical powers. All such
methods—unless specifically designed to be self-defeating
and so to reduce the ambition for power to absurdity—are
simply "ego trips" of a refined and highbrow order, but

71

often they produce such sensational short-run results that people are easily beguiled by the pseudo-gurus who tout them. Even Tibetan Buddhists, upon whom romanticists project their wildest fantasies of spiritual magic, make a clear distinction between the Way of Powers and the Way of Wisdom, insisting that the former, however far pursued, can never lead to Buddhahood.

The Way of Wisdom lies, therefore, in recognizing things which happen to you as your own karma—not as punishments for misdeeds or rewards for virtue (for there really is no "bad" or "good" karma), but as your own doing. For in this way you come to see that the real "you" includes both the controlled and the uncontrolled aspects of your experience. Much as we despise "primitives" for their animistic beliefs which regard mountains, rivers, trees, and animals as if they were people, they are on the right track because the animation of nature (rather than machinery) is a step in the direction of owning it as we own our brains and bodies, our appetites and dreams, for nature is our own unconscious activity. But almost every educated person has been trained to believe that everything outside the human skin is stupid and that air, water, earth, and fire are simply dead and witless substances. At the same time he has been trained to feel this whole dimension of "things that happen" as entirely disconnected from his own inner workings.

I am not, of course, suggesting that nature is purposeful in the same way as our conscious attention, with its verbal and numerical methods of calculation. Nature is purposeful only in and as man, just as it is yellow, long-necked, and spotted only in the giraffe. Otherwise, it has no more need of purposeful calculation than a snake needs legs. Nevertheless, it is undeniably intelligent. We ourselves did not get born on purpose; we do not plan our breath, nor calculate the circuitry of our brains, yet it is amazing how little we seem to realize that we would be incapable of purpose without these marvels of purposeless and involuntary construction. We are simply not used to the idea that there are forms of intelligence which do not use the linear, time-bound methods of conscious attention and scanning. Just as we do not confuse a televised image of the president with the president himself, we should not confuse our linear models of the world (in terms of words, numbers, or other strung-out signs) with the world itself.

I—and others—have been saying for years that destruction of the environment is based on contempt for everything outside the human skin, failure to see that as a field flowers, the planet peoples, and ignorance of the fact that the oceans, the air, and even the solar system are as much our vital organs as heart and stomach. We are not *in* nature; we *are* nature. But as masters of technical weapons we are fighting the environment as if we still believed ourselves to be strangers on the earth, sent down into this world from a purely abstract, ideational, and spiritual heaven. Oddly enough, people who call themselves naturalists and materialists are, when judged by their actions, the most devout abstractionists and the most dedicated violators of material.

What this comes to is that the spiritualist (or mentalist) and materialist (or mechanistic) philosophies are both on the same side. They represent opposed *concepts* of reality, and reality—nature—is not a concept. It is not material, if "material" means unspiritual, and not spiritual, if "spiritual" means nonmaterial. One could, perhaps, say that the sound of the waves is a spiritual experience and that pure mathematics is a physical operation of the nervous system. But the point is that our ideas about reality represent it but do not embrace it, since all conceptual views—spiritualism, materialism, voluntarism, determinism, vitalism, mechanism, etc.—are one-sided deviations from the Middle Way, where the wind is your own breath and your private thoughts are clouds in the sky.

November 1969 (transcription of a lecture)

We know that from time to time there arise among human beings people who seem to exude love as naturally as the sun gives out heat. These people, usually of enormous creative power, are the envy of us all, and, by and large, man's religions are attempts to cultivate that same power in ordinary people. Unfortunately, they often go about this task as one would attempt to make the tail wag the dog. I remember that when I was a small boy in school, I was enormously interested in being able to do my schoolwork properly. Everyone told me that I did not work hard enough, that I ought to work, but when I asked, "How do you work?" everybody shut up.

I was extremely puzzled. There were teachers who apparently knew how to work and who had attained considerable heights of scholarship. I thought that maybe I could learn "the secret" by copying their mannerisms. I would imitate the style of handwriting they used. I would use the same kind of pen. I would affect the same speech and gestures and, insofar as I could get around the school uniform, even clothing.

Spectrum of Love

(This was a private school in England, not a public school in America.)

None of this revealed the secret. I was, as it were, copying the outward symptoms and knew nothing of the inner fountain of being able to work. Exactly the same thing is true in the case of people who love. When we study the behavior of people who have the power of love within them, we can catalogue how they behave in various situations, and out of this catalogue formulate certain rules.

One of the peculiar things we notice about people who have this astonishing universal love is that they are often apt to play it rather cool on sexual love. The reason is that for them an erotic relationship with the external world operates between that world and every single nerve ending. Their whole organism—physical, psychological, and spiritual—is an erogenous zone. Their flow of love is not channeled as exclusively in the genital system as is most other people's. This is especially true in a culture such as ours, where for so many centuries that particular expression of love has been so marvelously repressed as to make it seem the most desirable. We have, as a result of two thousand years of repression, "sex on the brain." It's not always the right place for it.

People who exude love are in every way like rivers— they stream. And when they collect possessions and things that they like, they are apt to give them to other people. (Did you ever notice that when you give things away, you keep getting more? That, as you create a vacuum, more flows in?)

Having noticed this, the codifiers of loving behavior write that you should give to tax-deductible institutions and to the poor, and should be nice to people, that you should act towards your relatives and friends and indeed even enemies as if you loved them (even if you don't). For Christians and Jews and believers in God, there is a peculiarly difficult task enjoined upon us: namely, that "thou shalt love the Lord thy God," not only going through the motions externally, but with all your heart, with all your soul, and with all your mind. And that is of course very demanding indeed.

It is as if, for example, we admired the music of a certain composer and, having studied his style very thoroughly, we drew up rules of musical composition based upon the behavior of this composer. We then send our children to music school where they learn these rules in the hope that if they apply them, they will turn into first-class musicians, which they usually fail to do. Because what might be called the technique of music—as the technique of morals, as well as the technique of speech, of language —is very valuable because it gives you something to express. If you don't have anything to say, not even the greatest mastery of English will long stand you in good stead.

So the question and the puzzle remain: You cannot imitate this thing . . . there is no way of "getting" it, and yet it is absolutely essential that we have it. Obviously, the human race is not going to flourish harmoniously unless we are able to love each other. The question becomes: How do you get it? Is it something that you simply have to contract, like measles? Or, as theologians say, is it "a gift of divine grace" which somehow is dished out to some but not to others? And if there is no way of getting divine grace by anything you do, as the Calvinists aver, then hadn't we better just sit around and wait until something happens?

Surely, we can't be left in that sort of hopeless situation. There must be some way of getting "grace" or "divine charity" or "divine love"—some sort of way in which we can, as it were, open ourselves so as to become conduit pipes for the flow.

The more subtle preachers try to see if we can open ourselves and thus teach methods of meditation and spiritual discipline in the hope that we can contact this power. Less subtle preachers simply say you don't have enough faith or guts or will power: "If you only put your shoulder to the wheel and shoved, you would be an exemplar and a saint."

Actually, you may only be an extremely clever hypocrite. The whole history of religion is the history of the failure of preaching. Preaching is moral violence. When you deal with the so-called practical world, and people don't behave the way you wish they would, you get out the army or police force or "the big stick." And if those strike you as somewhat crude, you resort to giving lectures—"lectures" in the sense of solemn adjuration and exhortation to "behave better next time."

Many a parent says to the child, "Nice children love their mothers. And I'm sure you're a nice child. You ought to love your mother, not because I, your mother, say so, but because you really want to do so." One of the difficulties here is that none of us, in our heart of hearts, respects love which is not freely given. For example, you have an ailing parent, and you are a son or daughter who feels dutifully that he should look after his parents because they've done so much for him. But somehow, your living with your father or mother prevents you from having a home and a life of your own, and naturally you resent it. Your parents are well aware that you resent this, even if they pretend to ignore it. They therefore feel guilty that they have imposed upon your loyalty. You in turn can't really admit the fact that you resent them for getting sick, even though they couldn't help it. And therefore no one enjoys the relationship. It becomes a painful duty to be carried out.

The same thing would naturally happen if, a number of years after having (at the altar) made a solemn and terrible promise that you would love your wife or husband come what may forever and ever "until death do you part," suddenly you find that you really haven't the heart to do it any more. Then you feel guilty, and that you *ought* to love your wife and family.

The difficulty is this: You cannot, by any means, *teach* a selfish person to be *un*selfish. Whatever a selfish person does, whether it be giving his body to be burned, or giving all that he possesses to the poor, he will still do it in a selfish way of feeling, and with extreme cunning, marvelous self-deception, and deception of others. But the consequences of fake love are almost invariably destructive, because they build up resentment on the part of the person who does the fake loving, as well as on the part of those who are its recipients. (This may be why our foreign-aid program has been such a dismal failure.)

Now, of course, you may say that I am being impractical and might ask, "Well, do we just have to sit around and wait until we become inwardly converted and learn, through the grace of God or some other magic, how to love? In the meantime, do we do nothing about it, and conduct ourselves as selfishly as we feel?"

The first problem raised here is honesty. The Lord God says, at the beginning of things, "Thou shalt love the Lord thy God with all thy heart, with all thy soul, and with all thy mind." What appears to be a commandment is actually a challenge, or what in Zen Buddhism is called a *koan*, a spiritual *problem*. If you exercise yourself resolutely, and *try* to love God or your neighbor, you will find that you get more tangled up. You will realize increasingly that the reason you are attempting to obey this as a commandment is that you want to be the right kind of person.

But love is not a sort of rare commodity—everybody has it. Existence is love. Everybody has the force running. Perhaps the way in which you find the force of love operating in you is as a passionate like for booze or ice cream or automobiles or good-looking members of the opposite sex, or even of the same sex. But love is operating there. People, of course, tend to distinguish between various kinds of love. There are "good" kinds, such as divine charity, and there are allegedly "bad" kinds, such as "animal lust." But they are all forms of the same thing. They relate in much the same way as the colors of the spectrum produced by passing light through a prism. We might say that the red end of the spectrum of love is Dr. Freud's libido, and the violet end of the spectrum of love is *agape*, the divine love or divine charity. In the middle, the various yellows, blues, and greens are as friendship, human endearment, consideration.

Now it's said that selfish people "love themselves." I would say that that belies a misunderstanding of the whole thing: "yourself" is really something that is impossible to love. One obvious reason for this is that one's self, when you try to focus on it to love it or know it, is oddly elusive.

Let me illustrate why. Once there was a fish who lived in the great ocean, and because the water was transparent, and always conveniently got out of the way of his nose when he moved along, he didn't know he was in the ocean.

Well, one day the fish did a very dangerous thing, he began to *think*: "Surely I am a most remarkable being, since I can move around like this in the middle of empty space." Then the fish became confused because of *thinking* about moving and swimming, and he suddenly had an anxiety paroxysm and thought he had forgotten how. At that moment he looked down and saw the yawning chasm of the ocean depths, and he was terrified that he would drop. Then he thought: "If I could catch hold of my tail in my mouth, I could hold myself up." And so he curled himself up and snapped at his tail. Unfortunately, his spine wasn't quite supple enough, so he missed. As he went on trying to catch hold of his tail, the yawning black abyss below became ever more terrible, and he was brought to the edge of total nervous breakdown.

The fish was about to give up, when the ocean, which had been watching with mixed feelings of pity and amusement, said, "What are you doing?" "Oh," said the fish, "I'm terrified of falling into the deep dark abyss, and I'm trying to catch hold of my tail in my mouth to hold myself up." So the ocean said, "Well, you've been trying that for a long time now, and still you haven't fallen down. How come?" "Oh, of course, I haven't fallen down yet," said the fish, "because, because—I'm swimming!" "Well," came the reply, "I am the Great Ocean, in which you live and move and are able to be a fish, and I have given all of myself to you in which to swim, and I support you all the time you swim. But here you, instead of exploring the length, breadth, depth, and height of my expanse, are wasting your time pursuing your own end." From then on, the fish put his own end behind him (where it belonged) and set out to explore the ocean.

Well, that shows one of the reasons it's difficult to love yourself: Your "spine isn't quite supple enough."

Another reason is that "oneself," in the ordinary sense of one's ego, doesn't exist. It seems to exist, in a way, in the sense that the equator exists as an abstraction. The ego is not a psychological or physical organ, it's a social convention, like the equator, like the clock or the calendar, or like the dollar bill. These social conventions are abstractions which we agree to treat as if they did exist. We live in relation to the external world in just exactly the same way that one end of the stick exists in relation to the other end. The ends are indeed different, but they're of the same stick.

Likewise, there is a polar relationship between what you call your "self" and what you call "other." You couldn't experience your "self" unless you could experience "other," nor could you experience "other" unless you also had the experience of "self." We might say that we feel that one's "self" and the "other" are poles apart. Oddly, we use that phrase, "poles apart," to express extreme difference. But things that are "poles apart" are poles *of* something, as of a magnet, or a globe, and so are actually inseparable. What happens if you saw the south pole off a magnet with a hacksaw? The new end, opposite the original north pole, *becomes* the south pole, and the piece that was chopped off develops its own north pole. The poles are inseparable and generate each other.

So it is in the relationship between the "self" and the "other." Now, if you explore what you mean when you say you "love yourself," you will make the startling discovery that everything that you love is something that you thought was *other than* yourself, even if it be very ordinary things such as ice cream or booze. In the conventional sense, booze is not you. Nor is ice cream. It becomes "you," in a manner of speaking, when you consume it, but then you don't "have it" any more, so you look around for more in order to love it once again. But so long as you love it, it's never you. When you love people, however selfishly you love them (because of the pleasant sensations they give you), still, it is somebody *else* that you love. And as you inquire into this and follow honestly your own selfishness, many interesting transformations begin to occur in you.

One of the most interesting of these transformations is being directly and honestly "selfish." You stop deceiving people. A great deal of damage is done in practical human relations by saying that you love people, when what you mean is that you ought to (and don't). You give the impression, and people begin to expect things of you which you are never going to come through with.

You know of people to whom you say, "I like so-and-so, because with him or her, you always know where you are." It's impossible to impose on people like that. On the other hand, if you say, "Can I come and stay overnight with you?" and they don't want you, they'll reply, "I'm sorry, but I'm tired this weekend, and I'd rather not have you." Or "Some other time." Well, that's very refreshing. If I feel the person hasn't been quite honest with me, and I accept their hospitality, I'm always wondering if they would really prefer that I wasn't there.

But one doesn't always listen to one's inner voice: we often pretend that it's not there. That's unfortunate, because if you don't listen to your inner voice, you are not listening to your own wisdom and to your own love. You are becoming insensitive to it just as your hosts are trying to suppress the fact that, for the time being, they don't want your presence. Likewise, let's suppose that you are married and have an unwanted baby. It is profoundly disturbing to a child to have false love pretended to it. To begin with, the milk tastes wrong. The smell isn't right. The outward gesture is "Darling, I love you," but the smell is "You're a little bastard and a nuisance."

Very few of us can accept the idea that we don't love our children, because it seems to be unnatural. We say that mother-love is the most beautiful and natural thing in the world. But it isn't. It's relatively rare, and if you don't love your child, you confuse him or her. The child will respect you much more if you say, "Darling, you're a perfect nuisance, but I will look after you because I have to." Well, at least then everything is quite clear!

I found in personal relations of this kind a very wonderful rule: that you never, never show false emotions. You don't have to tell people exactly what you think "in no uncertain terms," as they say. But to fake emotions is destructive, especially in family matters and between husbands and wives or between lovers. It always comes to a bad end. Thus, on the occasions when, for personal friends, I perform marriage ceremonies, instead of saying, "I require and charge you both that you shall answer in the dreadful Day of Judgment, etc.," I say, "I require and charge you both that you shall never pretend to love one another when you don't." This is a gamble. It is likewise a gamble to trust yourself to come through with love.

But there is really no alternative.

Now to trust oneself to be capable of love or to bring up love—in other words, to function in a sociable way and in a creative way—is to take a risk, a gamble. You may not come through with it. In the same way, when you fall in love with somebody else, or form an association with someone else, and you trust them, they may as a matter of fact not fulfill your expectations. But that risk has to be taken. The alternative to taking that risk is much worse than trusting and being deceived.

When you say, "I will not trust other people, and I will not trust myself," what course remains? You have to resort to force. You have to employ stacks of policemen to protect you, and have to hold a club over yourself all the time, and say, "No, no. My nature is wayward, animal, perverse, fallen, grounded in sin." What then happens? When you refuse to take the gamble of trusting yourself to be capable of love, you become, if you will excuse this extremely graphic but nevertheless relevant simile, like a person who cannot trust himself to have bowel movements. Many children learn this from parents who do not trust them, and think they ought to have these movements in rhythm with the clock, which is a different kind of rhythm from that of the organism. People who cannot trust themselves to do even this take laxatives endlessly, as a result of which their whole system gets fouled up.

Exactly the same thing happens with people who can't trust themselves to go to sleep. They have to take all kinds of pills. And so also with people who can't trust themselves to love, and have to take all sorts of artificial and surgical measures to produce the effect of love for saving face. They become progressively more incapable of loving at all, and they create turmoil and misunderstanding and chaos in themselves and others and society.

In other words, to live, and to love, you have to take risks. There will be disappointments and failures and disasters as a result of taking these risks. But in the long run it will work out.

My point is that if you don't take these risks the results will be much worse than any imaginable kind of anarchy.

In tying up love in knots or in becoming incapable of it, you can't destroy this energy. When you won't love, or won't let it out, it emerges anyway in the form of self-destruction. *The alternative to self-love, in other words, is self-destruction.* Because you won't take the risk of loving yourself properly, you will be compelled instead to destroy yourself.

So, which would you rather have? Would you rather have a human race which isn't always very well controlled, and sometimes runs amok a little bit, but on the whole continues to exist, with a good deal of honesty and delight, when delight is available? Or would you rather have the whole human race blown to pieces and cleaned off the planet, reducing the whole thing to a nice, sterile rock with no dirty disease on it called life?

The essential point is to consider love as a spectrum. There is not, as it were, just nice love and nasty love, spiritual love and material love, mature affection on the one hand and infatuation on the other. These are all forms of the same energy. And you have to take it and let it grow where you find it. When you find only one of these forms existing, if at least you will water it, the rest will blossom as well. But the effectual prerequisite from the beginning is to let it have its way.

September 1969

Day by day the tragic "crisis of color" between black and white peoples (or should we say colored and discolored?) moves towards a terrifying showdown. Remote and lofty as such matters may seem (though I would call them basic), it is always important to look into the religious and metaphysical background of social disturbances which, in this case, looms rather large. Through Christianity, and to a lesser extent Judaism, the West has inherited certain associations of ideas and symbols as unique among world religions as they are absurd. Consider these two columns:

White	Black
Light	Darkness
Life	Death
Good	Evil
God	Devil

The avowed aim of popular Western religion is to retain column 1 and to get rid of column 2. Most other religions would transcend both. We, however, have been persuaded that the white aspect of the universe can be experienced and enjoyed with the contrast of the black.

Black and/or White

"For anyone who holds that 'God made the world,' the question, Why did He permit the existence in it of any evil, or that of the Evil One in whom all evil is personified, is altogether meaningless; one might as well enquire why He did not make a world without dimensions or one without temporal succession."
Ananda Coomaraswamy

Strictly speaking, Africans are no more black than Caucasians are white, but first the Caucasians and now the Africans have adopted "white" and "black" as proud and belligerent labels, implying an opposition cruder and more irreconcilable than greyish pink versus brown. Yet if you are proud and happy to be white, how do you *know* you are white? But for the existence of colored people, we would never have thought of ourselves as white, for in an all-white world being white carries no distinction, and we surely like to be "people of distinction."

A necessary part of having an effective personality seems to be membership in some elite in-group of religion, class, or race, some sect, coterie, club, gang, or secret society. Even one's own body looks—deceptively—like an isolated in-group of cells. But just about the most basic metaphysical principle that I know is simply that every inside involves an outside, and every outside an inside. They are different, yes, but quite inseparable. The only exceptions to this principle are such topological gimmicks as the Möbius strip and the Klein bottle, though here there is neither front nor back, inside nor outside. Thus the principle is transcended, not annulled.

> "Superior virtue is not conscious of itself as virtue, and so really is virtue. Inferior virtue cannot let go of being virtuous, and so is not virtue. Superior virtue does not seem to be busy, and yet there is nothing which it does not accomplish. Inferior virtue is always busy, and yet in the end leaves things undone."
>
> *Lao-tzu*

If then, I am to be "in," someone else must be "out," and consequently I owe him a debt of gratitude for the realization that I am "in." To congratulate myself, if I must, on being a white, saved Protestant, a hard-working, family-minded and solid citizen, what is more convenient than the peripheral presence of a class of black, thinly disguised heathens, of shiftless, philandering, and irresponsible *fellaheen*? If the description doesn't fit, it must be made to fit. Otherwise, no congratulations. If I must, at all costs, be right I cannot discover myself in that position unless someone else is wrong, or left.

But the debt of gratitude is seldom, if ever, recognized— just as it would hardly occur to us to thank the darkness for light, sinners for saints, or the open air for being indoors. We think of the "in" situation as more energetic and even more real than the "out," for everyone who is not right inside is left outside by default. Yet when certain outsiders "want in" by virtue of equal energy and intelligence, they are not so much left out as pushed out. However, the lack of recognition here goes much deeper than racial prejudice.

As you read these lines, it seems obvious that the black print is more significant, more worthy of attention, and thus somehow more real, more "the thing," than the white paper, and the same would be true if it were white print on black paper. The Gestalt theory of perception explains that in any figure/background situation, the figure captures our attention to the extent that it is relatively small and enclosed, or that it is moving against a still background. The figure is then "the thing," and the background is more or less ignored—even though the figure would be invisible without its contrast. Yet, in the accompanying picture of a Mexican blanket, do we have a black design on a white ground, or a white design on a black? And what about a zebra? Does it remind you of a yellow horse with black stripes, or a black horse with yellow stripes?

In the case of printed words on a page, it is clear that the words and not the page are what one is supposed to notice. But when two contrasting colors are equally distributed we seem to have a choice. On the other hand, what about stars in space? Although our modern common-sense view is that the stars are "the things," and space just inert nothingness, some of the ancients saw the sky as a firmament pierced with apertures into the light of heaven, and for a long time

From an IQ test: Fill in the appropriate word in the following sentence, "Up is to down as ———— is to left." My answer is "taken."

Correct solution: The zebra is an invisible horse, striped black and yellow so you can see it coming.

As the fish doesn't know water, man is ignorant of space. Consciousness is concerned only with changing and varying details; it ignores constants— especially constant backgrounds. Thus only very exceptional people are aware of what is basic to everything.

now astrophysicists have considered space as having "properties," such as curvature and expansion. Furthermore, the nuclear exploration of solids suggests that even a rock contains far more space than "matter," while "matter" itself seems to dissolve more and more into energy patterns. Suppose, for example, that space is in the same sort of relation to solids as the diaphragm of a loudspeaker to the various sounds which it produces. We attend to the sounds as such, hearing voices, instruments, or footsteps, ignoring their common source and background—the vibration of the diaphragm, which is, in this instance, the active principle, translating electrical impulses into sound.

Though one must be careful of analogizing too much in these matters, I am convinced that switching attention back and forth from figure to ground, regarding each in turn as "the thing," is a fruitful heuristic method, especially if one wants to understand the relation of contexts to individual events, of environmental processes to organisms, and of fields of force to the patterns which they contain. L. von Bertalanffy, in his "systems theory" of biology, has argued very strongly that every biological process must be understood both by microscopic analysis and in context with the physical situation in which it occurs. This should, perhaps, be obvious, but scientific method has hitherto been overbalanced toward the analytic approach to nature.

When we consider energy itself, the mutual interdependence of positive and negative, of "white" ons and "black" offs, is still more obvious because all energy is a vibration or pulsation, or a propagation of waves. Unless plus and minus, on and off, wave-crest and wave-trough alternate, there simply is no energy. It is therefore tempting to assume that all negative aspects of the universe imply and involve

90

the positive, and vice versa, in such a way that the notion of final and absolute blackness is as absurd as its opposite. But when the white/positive is seen as "the real thing" there is always the fear that light and life may at last be overcome by darkness and death. However, the notion of plus and minus as generating one another in an eternal rhythm is far less a strain on my credulity and imagination than the idea of a brief and mysterious firing of energy occurring once, and once only, in the black waste of the void.

But the assumption that the black or negative aspect of the world is as essential to life as the white or positive is against the common-sense of Western man. He believes, in general, that life is, and should be, a relentless effort of mind and muscle against all forces of decay, dissolution, and death. "Fight the good fight with all thy might." "Accentuate the positive." Life is therefore seen as an intrusion into the dark emptiness of space—a darkness with which light has nothing in common, and which will engulf it forever if effort and total vigilance are not maintained. In one sense, this is a philosophy of nihilism in that it sees darkness and nonbeing as the truly basic and enduring reality—against which life is a magnificent though ultimately futile gesture. Unless, of course, there is some kind of God who exists necessarily and therefore *effortlessly* for all eternity. But if such a God is not merely the dark void, which is supremely effortless, He (or It) must somehow comprise or transcend the dark/light polarity. It would then be impossible to engulf or annihilate God, for He/She would be the black/white whole with no opposition.

My own feeling is that the universe is just that sort of arrangement, and that it is not actually chopped up into a

Must you see this image as either (white) a chalice, or as (black) two faces in profile about to kiss? Are the two interpretations mutually exclusive, or can you see them simultaneously with the idea that this is a loving-cup?

"The precious . . . uniqueness which the human individual claims is conferred on him not by possession of an immortal soul but by possession of a mortal body. . . . If death gives life individuality and if man is the organism which represses death, then man is the organism which represses his own individuality."
Norman O. Brown, *Life Against Death*

91

multitude of separate bits. It is an arrangement, or pattern, in which every so-called part is a function of the whole. Thus the Western attitude of being alive by virtue of being *against* death and darkness is not only naive but also destructive and violent. Its major technological achievement is the equipment for destroying the planet. It knows nothing of judo, the gentle way of getting where you want to go by going along with the movements of nature, using, say, gravity as a sailor uses the wind.

Every object in this universe is falling, gravitationally, but there is no concrete floor under the system upon which it can crash! The expert in judo gets the feeling that all his actions are "falling," and when he uses muscle he never strains. When he climbs a hill, he has the feeling that it is lifting him, for he takes it one step at a time and does not fight with it. He is never uptight because he is not afraid of the negative aspect of the world. He knows that it cannot destroy existence, because existence-energy is being/nothing, on/off, now you see it, now you don't. And—since the world has no truly separate parts—the only final and fundamental "I" or "Self" that we have is the whole thing.

The WASP attitude to the black world is, then, only a symptom of a state of consciousness which does not see the universe as a whole, which feels, quite one-sidedly, that the white design is the figure, "the thing," the reality, and the black background the evil, the nothing, the denial of life. So, too, it feels the individual person as isolated and disconnected from that essential background which we call "the other" or the external world. As the in-group does not acknowledge its dependence on the out-group, the life inside the skin has no sensation of being one with the life outside the skin. . . . But I have no self except everything

"Considered in its physical, concrete reality, the stuff of the universe cannot divide itself but, as a kind of gigantic 'atom,' it forms in its totality . . . the only real indivisible. The farther and more deeply we penetrate into matter by means of increasingly powerful methods, the more we are confounded by the interdependence of its parts. . . . It is impossible to cut into this network, to isolate a portion without it becoming frayed and unravelled at all its edges."
Teilhard de Chardin, *The Phenomenon of Man*

which is happening, and it sees itself from all the different standpoints called sentient beings.

We must go to the roots of a problem and not invest too much energy fiddling with the symptoms. We shall never get whites and blacks, or Orientals and Occidentals, to unite by trying to tie the different branches of the human tree together with string. Attention must instead be shifted to the stem and the root, where, under the surface, we are one. It will take much less time.

"When everyone recognizes beauty as beautiful, then there is ugliness. When everyone recognizes goodness as good, then there is evil. Thus being and non-being arise mutually. Easy and difficult are mutually implied. Short and long are mutually contrasted. High and low are mutually posited." *Lao-tzu*

93

May 1971

Whatever happened to the hippies? During the late sixties one had the impression that the ordinarily drab scene of American life was about to blossom into an easygoing colorful exuberance. Men seemed sure enough of their masculinity to abandon their customarily uptight machismo styles of dress and bearing, to let their hair down, to sing and wear jewelry, and to dress with imaginative elegance. It seemed that a positive life-style was being proposed as a less hectic and less expensive alternative to suburbia's conspicuous consumption of uniformly slick plastic hardware. The various forms of rock music showed possibilities of a legitimate development of the Western tradition which had come to a halt in the silences of John Cage and the electronic howls of *musique concrète*. Articulate glory seemed to be returning to Western art through the psychedelic painters. There were even prospects of a truly swinging religion with meditation, chanting, and joyous rituals, unorganized and set free from the unproductive guilt hangups of the Judeo-Christian conscience.

Consider the Lilies

But judging from Sausalito, California, as one of the hearts of the Movement, the hippies and flower-children have turned back into something even scruffier than beatniks. The long hair is tangled and snarled, and the blue denims patched and frayed. The beads and jewelry have been pawned, and the kapok is coming out of the pads. The attitude is silent—even surly—and the music has just turned up the volume. Hardly anyone dances at the Fillmore; they just sit. The rich verve of the *San Francisco Oracle* has disappeared from the ever more paranoid, violent, and funky underground press. "Love" has become "fuck." . . . But who needs it when personal style is contrived ugliness, and the girls manage to look like peasant women from some depressed area of Russia.

This sagging of spirits may reflect simple depression at the endless and sickening war, at the realization that it may be too late to do anything about ecological catastrophe, and at the difficulty of finding employment even in the sterile busywork of government and the big corporations. The temptation to free enterprise in dope is almost irresistible, but there can be too much pot—like too much booze or too much religion—and the result is not profound mystical contemplation but the most ordinary lethargy. (If the government wants to keep the people docile and avoid violence in the streets, it might note that lawn order follows from legalized grass.)

Furthermore, the exuberant "psychedelic" style went commercial and invaded the Establishment, but somehow this very success was taken as a failure. One wonders, therefore, whether the Movement, the Consciousness III people, want to woo the squares or simply to be their obedient reverse-image, just doing their opposite. Isn't it yet clear that originality and spontaneity are not being merely anti-conventional?

More and more, however, the professed philsophy is ecological concern, and there has indeed been an appreciable migration of hippies from the streets to the countryside in an attempt to love and cultivate the earth at first hand. Yet "charity begins at home" with love of one's own psychophysical organism (as distinct from conceptual ego) and of ordinary physical things. If the earth is man's extended body, to be loved and respected as one's own body, those who do no greening of themselves will hardly bring about the greening of America.

The idea of "greening" involves color, flowering, freshness of spring, and—above all—respect for what is organic and vegetative as distinct from the mechanical and metallic. As things are now going there is a real possibility that intelligence may survive on this planet only in the form of self-maintaining and self-reproducing steady-state electronic mechanisms, having no need for atmosphere and no feeling or emotions to obstruct their relentless efficiency. In such forms, abstract thought, logic, mathematics, and physics could continue to flourish on the planet, and some would see in this a triumph of purely spiritual principles over the trammels of the flesh. This would be a consistent direction of evolution for a species which confuses the world as described, in terms of linearly arranged word and number symbols, with the world itself; which goes on to value the symbolic more than the real (e.g., money more than real wealth and nations more than people), and which would compel the wiggly, lilting, and curvaceous forms of nature to get straightened out, squared away, and cleaned up.

I could make a strong, if not conclusive, case for the idea

that plants are more intelligent than people—more beautiful, more pacific, more ingenious in their ways of reproduction, more at home in their surroundings, and even more sensitive. Why, we even use flower-forms as our symbols of the divine when the human face reminds us too much of ourselves—the Hindu-Buddhist mandala, the golden lotus, and the Mystic Rose in Dante's vision of Paradise. Nothing else reminds us so much of a star with a living heart.

I wish, then, that hippies would once again consider the lilies—for the very reason that they are frail and frivolous, gentle and inconsequential, and thus have those very qualities of vegetative wisdom so despised by those who have wills of iron and nerves of steel to fight the good fight and run the straight race. As Lao-tzu put it two thousand years ago:

> Man at his birth is supple and tender, but in death he is rigid and hard.
> Plants when young are sinuous and moist, but when old are brittle and dry.
> Thus suppleness and tenderness are signs of life,
> While rigidity and hardness are signs of death.

For I feel that we would go better with this wiggly world if we thought in terms of roots and branches, vines and creepers, fronds and fiber, rather than in sterile angularities of metal and quartz in which the genius of life has not yet arisen, and in which energy may stutter and hum but has not yet learned to feel.

At least then let me hope—dear children—that there are seeds in your dirty fingernails, and that you will again come out with flowers.

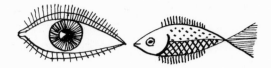

October 1970

"To come down to earth" is, in ordinary speech, to get to reality, to face the facts, and to be practical. On the other hand, "to have your head in the clouds" is to be a dreamer and a fantast, though oddly and curiously, the Christian notion of heaven, the abode of God and therefore the seat of ultimate reality, is traditionally symbolized as a situation where everyone floats in the sky. As a child, I remember singing a religious ditty, or hymn, which ran—

> A charge to keep I have,
>   A God to glorify,
> A never-dying soul to save,
>   And fit it for the sky.

Hardly anyone seems to realize that Earth has always been in the sky and that space is just as real as anything solid. Density and expansion are two poles of the same spectrum, like red and purple.

For a long time—of all the civilizations of the West —the United States has both prided itself and has been accused by others of being materialistic, although

What on Earth Are We Doing?

we ourselves call it being practical. When it really "comes down to earth," to the nitty-gritty, being practical is making money, and yet nothing could be more abstract, gaseous, and insubstantial than the banking-bookkeeping system known as money. Gold, silver, dollar bills, and credit cards are useless in the wilderness—as compared with knowing how to use a bow for hunting, how to make fire and cook, how to cultivate plants and herbs, or how to fish and sail a ship. Should Con Edison fail, P.G.&E. collapse, and Standard Oil explode or gas itself to death, most of us would be helpless—and all that could rather easily happen. What is real, if you have decided to live in the dimension of space and time, is muscle and nerve.

So we down-to-earth, gutsy, tough, realistic, and practical types have just been squandering billions of dollars and unimaginable amounts of energy, nerve-work, and materials in whizzing off to the moon to discover, as astronomers knew before, that it was just a dreary slag heap. This is the true, original and scientifically etymological meaning of being lunatics. Crying for the moon.

I have imagined a speech to be made by the president of the United States, perhaps by Richard Nixon, in which he reports that he has made a very careful survey of the desires and goals of his "silent majority," since this is his duty as their representative. He finds that they would like to return the Negroes to virtual slavery, to repeal the Bill of Rights, to confine all long-haired youths and obstreperous college students to concentration camps, to reduce taxation, to reaffirm states' rights and diminish the authority of federal government, to wipe all "gooks" in Southeast Asia off the map, and to subdue or annihilate the entire populations of China and Russia. Naturally, therefore, he goes on to say, as a good businessman and your humble servant I have had to make an estimate of the cost of this enterprise, not only in terms of money, but also in terms of time, trouble, energy, and nuclear fallout. I am sorry to say, he remarks, that if you want your government to control China, I will have to send *you* there to do it, and you will have to put up with chop suey instead of sirloin steaks and apple pie. Something will also have to be done about the amazing piles of rotting and stinking corpses, lest diseases should be spread all over the earth. The statistics, he goes on to say, are showing us that the boys we are sending to Vietnam are 75 percent nutty on marijuana and have contracted a brand of gonorrhea which doesn't get spiflicated by our antibiotics. Also, since the air currents of the upper atmosphere drift generally eastwards, the fallout of nuclear bombs dropped on China will eventually reach us, and poison our American mothers' milk with strontium-90 as it is already poisoned with DDT. I have also, he would say, had my accountants going over the figures on what it would involve to put the niggers in gas chambers or jails, and I am extremely sorry to say, my dear and loyal people, that you would have some embarrassment in paying the bills.

So what is the matter with us? The basic problem of civilization, whether it is American, German, British, Chinese, or Japanese, is that we confuse our systems of symbols and descriptions with the real, or natural, world, the universe represented with the universe present, the money with the wealth, the figures with the facts, the thoughts with the things, the ideas with the events, the ego with the organism, and the map with the territory. It is actually impossible to explain this verbally because, in writing or talking, one is still in the dimension of symbols, even

101

though using physical noises and marks on paper—and the very notion that such energy forms are "physical," material, and real is in turn merely a philosophical concept which is, again, a symbol. Thus the word "water" is itself undrinkable, and the formula H_2O will not float a ship.

Consider the difference between the two types of globe-maps of planet Earth, the physical and the political. The first is a marvelous wiggly affair, blue, green, brown, yellow, and occasionally white. The second, especially on the North American continent, is angrily scratched across with straight lines, and the one earth (and we should not forget the one air) covered with patches of contrasting colors to identify the domains of differing bands of gangsters. Which of the two more closely resembles Earth as seen from outer space?

Civilized human beings, and Westerners in particular, are always trying to straighten things out and put them in rectilinear boxes. This arises from the Greek superstition that there are three dimensions of space and from Euclid's brutally oversimplified fantasies of a world consisting of points, lines, surfaces, circles, and cubes. It is hard to persuade an educated Westerner that Euclid was simply a fantast and that his so-called geometry had nothing to do with measuring the earth, but only with working out the rules of his own rather rigid and simple mind. Earth wiggles, water streams and waves, and nature in general dances and swings, but Euclid's mind never reached the biological level. It stopped at the primitively crystalline stage of evolution. This is why generation after generation of schoolchildren have been bamboozled into the notion that a straight line is simpler, and thus more intelligible, than a wiggle. Ever after, we have been trying to subjugate all experience, knowledge, and action to the supposed clarity and intelligibility of straight lines.

Water, even light, and indeed all forms of energy follow gravity, the line of least resistance, and this is why space itself is said to be curved. $E = MC^2$ really means that energy is gravity. Newton, Einstein, and even many physicists today cannot understand this because they think of energy as a force busting through obstacles in an attempt to follow a straight line. Under some circumstances a straight line may be the shortest, and least fatiguing, distance between two points. But it's no fun to follow the "straight and narrow way." Is the River of Life itself a mere canal? In San Francisco we have built roads going straight up hills, though no experienced mountaineer would dream of climbing to the summit of Everest along a straight line.

The combination of Euclidean geometry, Roman law (and roads), and Protestant ethics gives us the impression that it is quite definitely immoral to follow the line of least resistance. Be a man. Stand up. But can you *will* an erection? Personally, I go on all fours when I cross a fallen tree high above a stream—not being afraid to sully my hands (that is, to soil them) nor to exercise the power of humility, of humus—the earth. I have no faith in the fetish of being perpetually and compulsively upright, because it is an Euclidean illusion to think that heaven is up and hell is down, and that all evils began with the fall of man. After all, one falls in love—and thereby continues the stream of life. A great mind is also considered "profound" because it plumbs the depths of things.

Furthermore, especially in philosophy and the sciences, we use words as a way of putting everything in boxes, or classes. Is you is or is you ain't? Animal, vegetable, or mineral? True or false? Why, to answer those tests they even print boxes on the questionnaire! The whole virtue of tidiness is to have things put away in boxes, and thus have them conformed in Euclidean principles, and this compulsion lies at the root of interminable fights between parents and children. My wife and I have a superintelligent Siamese cat, named Solstice, with whom I communicate in fake declamatory Japanese, yet his intelligence operates without the least attention to Euclid. We have never *trained* him to do anything except use a sandbox and to stay off tables, but he will accompany us on a hike in the hills, leaping and whizzing back and forth, and coming when called as well as a dog. It is just that the organism, the whole pattern of nerve and muscle, is more complex and intelligent than logical systems of arithmetic, geometry and grammar—which are in fact nothing but inferior ritual.

Life itself dances, for what else are trees, ferns, butterflies, and snakes but elaborate forms of dancing? Even wood and bones show, in their structure, the characteristic patterns of flowing water, which (as Lao-tzu pointed out in 400 B.C.) derives its incredible power by following gravity and seeking that "lowest level which all men abhor." When I dance I do not think-count my steps, and some women say I have no sense of rhythm, but I have a daughter who (without ever having taken lessons in dancing) can follow me as if she were my shadow or I were hers. The whole secret of life and of creative energy consists in flowing with gravity. Even when he leaps and bounces our cat is going with it. This is the way the whole earth and everything in the universe beehives.*

* Harrumph! Excuse the pun, but it is important, because bees live in hexagonal as distinct from quadrilateral structures, and this is the nat-

But man is making a mess of the earth because he is using his Euclidean intellect instead of his organic brain. He is symbolizing and describing nature along the straight or by the curve of the simplistic circle, and though such mathematicians as topologists and matrix theorists are capable of much more sophisticated operations, the averagely civilized Western person still figures the world according to Euclid and to the arithmetic of decimation. In this time of ecological crisis we are therefore into a big fight. On the one hand, there are people known as straight, regular, square (and there are also cubes and tesseracts), classified, degreed, graduated, and moneyed, who live in little boxes made of ticky-tacky, cultivate lawn order, and want to get things ironed out in nothing flat. On the other, there are bohemians, nuts, bums, freaks, eccentrics, beatifics, wholly-men, courtesans, vagrants, and hippies (a name which ought to have something to do with the dangerous curves of women's hips), who want to experience the universe in a groovy, swinging, ecstatic, syncopated, rock-and-rolling, mind-blown, turned-on, and far-out way.

The first group emulate and admire the behavior of machines; they think like machines, and thus have made the machines in their own image. It has conquered them and taken them over. The second go for the more wiggly and squishy organization of plants and animals, and it is thus that, in the eyes of the first, they are unclean, sloppy,

---

ural way in which all things, such as bubbles and pebbles, congregate, nestling into each other by gravity. It will follow, because 2 x 6 is 12, that—as Buckminster Fuller has pointed out—a number-system to the base 12 (duodecimal) is closer to nature than one to the base 10 (decimal). For 12 is divisible by both 2 and 3, whereas 10 is not. After all, we use the base 12 for measuring circles and spheres and time, and so can "think circles" around people who use only meters. The world is better duodecimalized than decimated.

feckless, messy, bestial, and even shitty—because their way of life is not mechanical but biological. Thus they refuse absolutely to be regimented—and in this connection it should be pointed out to the first group that their regimental military tactics have thus far failed against those unspeakable guerrilla "gooks" of North Vietnam. The only way of getting a military victory in Vietnam would be to send in Mr. Clean with nuclear weapons and bulldozers and scour the place down to good old rock-of-ages. But that would hardly be fighting fair, in the ancient and honorable traditions of chivalry. (Remember, incidentally, the tactics used by the American revolutionaries against the redcoats.)

Let us look, now, at some of the things which the Euclidean mind has done to our everyday life. It is increasingly difficult to buy real food. We are beginning to eat machinery. Most bread is plastic froth. Chickens taste of papier-mâché, because they are fed on chemicals and bred in immense penitentiaries. Milk is homogenized, and real cream is hardly to be found. More and more, cheese is a processed and textureless glob. There are projects now for growing cubic tomatoes, to be more easily packed in cubic boxes, to be stored in cubic warehouses; for featherless chickens, to eliminate the nuisance of plucking; for shell-less eggs, sold in pocketed plastic bags; and for branchless trees, chemically stained from birth, from which to make straight lumber without knots or wiggles.

Although we all realize that monotony is boring, almost every form of industrial work—banking, accounting, mass-producing—is monotonous, and most people are paid simply for putting up with monotony, for arranging things in boxes, for recording these arrangements on squared and columned sheets of paper, or for welding and drilling innumerable I-beams together for making colossal concrete or glass-walled boxes wherein myriads of others can pursue these dreary routines. For what? For absolutely necessary but abstract and inedible money, wherewith to purchase a box in which to live, another box in which to go about (look at almost any brand of car from above), and to acquire boxed food which tastes more and more as if its constituent particles were boxes instead of cells.

The tycoons, politicians, and gangsters who manage this operation, whether in Russia, China, West Germany, or the United States, are not happy. By and large they are vulgar men who do not know chalk from cheese, who know very well what they hate and fear, but haven't the least idea of what they love—except statistical records called money. Some of them have celebrated libraries of pornography. Some have plush harems of frigid girls. Some have yachts and jet planes in which to go somewhere just like the place from which they began. Some have great stables of horses for the merely mathematical purpose of betting on races. They live in constant terror of thievery, revolution, competition, impotence, cancer, and rising taxation.

If I sound like a preacher or biblical prophet, let us take a look at regular religion, whose ministry makes at least ritual murmurs against the rich and the powerful—for the wrong reasons. For the trouble with our rich and powerful people is not so much that they are wicked, but that they do not enjoy themselves. A square can't have a ball, and the great problem of philosophy is not so much to square the circle as circle the square. For our religions are uptight and anal-retentive, and even Freud thought of the "reality-principle," as distinct from the "pleasure-principle," as a form of Euclidean order. Oddly, on the other hand, it is said of Jesus that when confronted with human suffering "the bowels of his compassion" were moved.

Our religious observances consist almost entirely of talk —"about it and about"— about obeying commandments and about believing in verbalized statements or creeds presuming to define the ineffable. Virtually nothing is done to encourage any form of silent, nonverbal meditation or yoga wherein the eternal is experienced and not merely discussed. Many Christians will even assert that, save under the most extraordinary circumstances, you cannot experience God until you are dead, and thus are terrified of "cosmic consciousness" or mystical experience as something close to madness. Because, then, the religion is verbal the opposition is also just verbal, and our atheists are as phony as our believers. It is a terrible and notorious truth of history that no one has ever been taught how to love by a sermon, for all sermonically based love is simply disguised guilt, which arouses resentment in the recipient. If love can be inspired by anything symbolic, it has to be brought out by poetry—that is, by words used as music

Real religion has nothing to do with words. It is a silent, effortless, and fascinated concentration on the basic energy, the fundamental and musical vibration of the world— which, as Saint Thomas Aquinas might have said, "is what all men call God." You do religion as you breathe easily, slowly, and delightedly, or listen intently to a bird singing at dawn, or ride a surfboard on the exact dynamic center of an immense wave. Ali Akbar Khan, a splendid rollicking man who is the acknowledged master of Indian music— along with his noble and gentler peer Ravi Shankar—has said that the whole art of music consists in understanding one tone. That is religion in its supreme form, and that is why yogis will chant or hum the syllable OM or AUM (or Zen Buddhists the sound MU) because it comprises the entire range of voice from the throat to the lips. You can do it just as well with AMEN (meaning "Let It Be") if you have to disguise yourself as a Christian or Jew, or ALLAH if you are a Muslim. By such means we experience life as it actually is, as beyond the ways in which it is merely measured and described and calculated (reduced to stones) in our various systems of symbols. In the end you find out that you yourself are nothing other than that basic and timeless energy. And, by the way, when Saint Thomas was an old man he had such an experience in the midst of celebrating the Mass, whereas he said that all the theology he had written was mere straw.

When you find that out, you don't give a damn about status, fancy possessions, hoards of money, being embalmed and buried in a bronze casket, and living a neatly geometrized life. Enough is as good as a feast. You don't even quake with anxiety about survival. As Confucius put it, "A man who understands the Tao [the Course of Nature] in the morning may die without regret in the evening." When I explain this to Americans they invariably ask, "But doesn't this imply a merely passive attitude to life?" That is because they have been brought up on such hymns as

> Awake, my soul, stretch ev'ry nerve,
>   And press with vigor on;
> A heav'nly race demands thy zeal,
>   And an immortal crown.

And also "Onward Christian soldiers, marching as to war." Besides, who wants an immortal crown? I can't imagine anything more like hell than having to wear a golden ring of spikes and being flattered by angels forever.

I simply do not understand the goals and rewards of the Western Way of Life, apart from such side-effects of the project as anesthesia for dentistry (which can just as well be effected by hypnosis). What is the point of Progress if the food is tasteless, the housing absurd, the clothing uncomfortable, the religion just talk, the air poisoned by Cadillacs, the work boring, the sex uptight and mechanical, the earth clobbered with concrete, and the water so chemicalized that even the fish are abandoning existence? Recently, I have been asking questions that really need no answer. Who wants to serve in a police vice squad, spending hours peeking into men's johns to detect acts of homosexuality? Who wants a job as a debt-collection agent, spending his whole day being nasty to people? What sort of person voluntarily serves as a prison guard or hangman? Also, alas, one might ask what kind of individual would want to spend millions of dollars to become president of the United States, never away from the telephone, guarded around the clock by agents of the Secret Service, reading tomes of amazingly uninteresting documents, and being accompanied day and night by a warrant officer carrying a black bag containing the mechanisms to set off the atomic bomb?

We believe that all such occupations, dreary or dangerous as they may be, are exercises of high responsibility and even of glory, despite the maxim that "the paths of glory lead but to the grave." But what is their actual end and purpose? Towards what is Progress? In fact, what on Earth are we doing? No one has even the ghost of a notion, save perhaps a few simple-minded people who live to smell flowers, to listen to the sea, to watch trees in the wind, to climb mountains, to eat *pâté de veau en croûte,* to drink the Malvasia wine from Ruby Hill, and to cuddle up with a lovely woman—and such pursuits are not really expensive, as compared with the trillions spent on the Kingdom, the Power, and the Glory.

Warfare is, and has been for many centuries, the major waste of Earth's resources, and, as time goes on, people fight with each other for less and less sensible reasons. Although I have a very slight suspicion that we are fighting in Vietnam to gain control of the world's best supply of opium, no competent strategist would completely obliterate the flora, fauna, and women of a country which he intends to possess. He might, indeed, be greedy—but he should not compound this vice with stupidity. The energy and material which we have all squandered on making war since even 1914 could have warmed, fed, and clothed everyone on Earth, but we go about this atrocious squandering in the name of such immaterial and irrelevant fantasies as religion, honor, ideology, progress, racial purity, and patriotism—the last being not love of one's country but of the *idea* of one's country, of the mere image, the flag, the crown, the icon of Lenin, Mao's little red book, the cross, the crescent, the swastika, and other such absurd baubles.

Much of the trouble is that we confuse peoples, as living organisms, with their different ways of babbling or gesturing—and how monotonous Earth would be if we all did it the same way. And thus we imagine that there are really such creatures as Americans and Russians, Greeks and Romans, Indians and Chinese, Easterners and Westerners, Jews and Arabs, Christians and heathens. There are NOT. All this is babble, though babble is great fun when taken

111

as such and not confused with a High, Solemn, Pompous, and Serious Something. It is not well known that all the best angels wear their haloes jauntily, over one ear. Even the fascinating investigations of science have become a pest since academic scientists have taken themselves seriously, like theologians, humming and hawing, bumbling and rumbling, about whether so-and-so's hypotheses are really, truly, and absolutely *sound*.

Which is often all that they are. *Vox, et praeterea nihil.*

It is an old proverb that "travel broadens the mind," which used to be true insofar as it revealed the vast lands and waters of Earth and the variety of its cultures, languages, animals, and plants. But now travel is narrowing the world, because we can proceed almost instantly in sealed tubes from one "place" to another—in such a way that all these places are swiftly becoming the same place—New York, Los Angeles, Tokyo, New Delhi, Tel Aviv, Paris, London, each with identical Hilton-type boxes—and all the aborigines fouling their air with gasoline fumes and making themselves uncomfortable in business suits, presumably to imitate our own symbolism of success and status in life. By the time we get supersonic airlines we shall just go bang, bang, bang from one Euclidean point to another, living in a state of position without magnitude. When I was last in Kyoto I ran into some leggy and raucous blondes from Texas who were in there for four hours, off a plane landed in Osaka, and wanted to know "what to see"—though their state of mind prevented them from seeing anything except the American bar of the International Hotel, where they sat boasting that just at any time l'il ole Tayaxass could abdicate from the United States. (There are people in that State who believe so fervently in lawn order that they spray their sun-browned grass with green paint.)

Obviously, one of the major confusions of symbol with reality lies in a dimension of human relations called Sex— as pointed out long ago by Marshall McLuhan in a witty commentary on advertising, *The Mechanical Bride,* in which he showed that women were being reduced to machines like those inflatable or hot-water-bottle life-size girls made of rubber or plastic which can be obtained in Kobe or Marseilles, and are said to be used by merchant seamen on long and lonely voyages. He showed how women had been chopped into detachable and even replaceable parts, like cars—the coiffure, the lips, the bosoms, the waist, the hips, the buttocks, or the legs—each being a point of fetishistic concentration. The current ideal of feminine beauty is a skinny lass with long, straight hair, overblown bosoms, a narrow waist, and a moderately protrusive bottom. But the girls of Renoir and Ingres were pleasingly plump, and the prehistoric Venus-images of Western Europe had such exaggeratedly female figures that we would now think of them as having elephantiasis. Get yourself a new model.

For the life-ideal of power-crazy men is (and the word is not insignificant) screwing a plastic woman. She doesn't talk back. She lies perfectly still. She will assume any position you want and be treated in any way. In fact, when it comes down to it, the whole enterprise of technology is to turn all nature into a plastic woman—a mass of completely obedient and predictable stuff. She's a dame, a broad, a bag, a chick, a cunt, an old lady, or a piece of ass.

Now the political world is very largely ruled by men who, like Julius Caesar, cannot make up their minds whether to be heterosexual or homosexual. Somehow they are ashamed to be frankly both, and therefore to be truly sure that they are *men* put on an immense show of masculinity. Western Europe and North America are highly overpopulated with such males. They screw dames galore and count the numbers as an ace fighter pilot puts symbols of enemy aircraft shot down on his fuselage. But their real sexual kick is in spearing, shooting, or torturing other males, whom they secretly love—because they lust over the convulsions of men dying, for the sadomasochistic type has his neurological wires crossed and mixes the convulsions of orgasm with those of agony (a useful trick if, and only if, you run into inevitable pain). Thus the merely symbolic necessity of being a real Man is manifested, not only in warfare, but also in pseudo-athletics (such as boxing, as distinct from judo), in American football, and in bullfighting. In all such pretentious activities force is used to go against gravity, the wind, and the grain.

Why not, instead, lust over the syncopated convulsions of your wife or girlfriend in bed, when you get her into the genuine ecstasy of the witch riding on the broom? To me, this is far more manly than smashing and destroying other people and their property, killing wild animals that you neither need nor use for food, or thundering along racetracks in four-wheeled phalluses. Why not go in for something like gliding, sailing, swimming, or even dancing? Incidentally, I have noticed that these Caesar fellows *cannot* dance, except in the most stilted and formal way, because they will not permit their hips to swing freely—imagining this to be a strictly feminine gesture. As boys they were taught to stand at attention, to form fours, to march in columns (stamping or goose-stepping), to handle rifles with

grotesque jerks, and, in short, to practice the most ineffi-
cient form of military discipline ever invented. Indeed, they
win battles (at immense cost of life and material, as in the
holocausts of World War I) but they lose wars, and today
almost all wars are lost.

Thus the traditional military style is merely symbolic
manhood. A marching column is easily enfiladed or bombed.
American soldiers in Vietnam jungles are immediately
scented out by their soapy smell, and spotted by their shiny
white faces. Likewise, military people wear trussed-up uni-
forms and boots which make it impossible to run with any
speed, or to slide, wiggle, and wangle. Note that all such
undulative motions are considered a sort of cheating—as
devious, as not standing up to the enemy out there in front
like a man—where you make a splendid target. Remember
those absurd Japanese *banzai* charges of World War II,
which were simply suicidal displays of samurai machismo,
because they were nothing more than running straight into
the immense firepower of American industry.

Dulce et decorum est pro patria mori—sweet and de-
corous it is to die for one's country—echoed by that very
articulate and pompous Lord Macaulay:

> Then out spake brave Horatius,
> The Captain of the Gate:
> "To every man upon this earth
> Death cometh soon or late.
> And how can man die better
> Than by facing fearful odds,
> For the ashes of his fathers
> And the temples of his Gods?"

So one gives one's life for cremated bodies in columbaria
and for symbolic structures of stone. If I were asked to

115

preach a sermon at the laying of a foundation stone for a church, I would take as my text the words of Jesus, "If a man's son ask him bread, will he give him a stone?" Of course. It is now called the generation gap.

Amerindians know that stones are live, but in our culture the stone, the tombstone, represents death—and thus supreme manliness consists in getting dramatically killed on a point of honor, which is for a merely verbal and symbolic issue. And, ironically, Bob Dylan mocks it all with his marvelous double-talk, "Ever'body's gotta get stoned." We therefore come back to the point that what we call manliness, valor, heroism, and courage consist in a fascination for death. If you pass the test they will put your name on a big stone war memorial, so that you can be hard and erect forever—as was not always so easy in life.

Wasn't it Voltaire who said, *"Il faut cultiver notre jardin"*—it is necessary that we cultivate our gardens? But here we *pay* farmers not to work, or to destroy or merely hoard their crops. For our problem is that we do not truly love the vegetable, lush, and wiggly world—and deem it beneath dignity to play with it, because we are fascinated and hypnotized with the mass erection of boxes and with straightening things out. Much of this began because our farming people had a rigid, antisexual religion, based on an elegantly mistranslated book, *The Bible,* so that their children fled for relief to the bright lights and distractions of the cities where they could find girls who would play games. But lack of love for the vegetative, subtle, cthonic, pagan, and sexy aspect of the world means death. The cry, "Back to Nature!" used to be derided as unrealistic sentimentality, but I am wondering if it is not becoming an urgent necessity. In A.D. 40 the wise emperor of Rome, Augustus, was

116

worried about the migration of people to the cities, and persuaded Virgil to write the celebrated verse:

> *O fortunatos nimium, sua si bona norint,*
> *   agricolas! . . .*
> Blest, aye, blest to excess: knew they
>   how goodly the portion Earth giveth
>   her farmers, who, afield where war's
>   din is heard not,
> Find ready there the pleasures which
>   nature most justly affords them.

After long practice of something between yoga and the Zen Buddhist style of meditation, I have at last come to see that there is nothing degrading or boring in soiling my hands. As a writer, intellectual, and sedentary worker, I am not as strong as I should be for the work of gardening—though I don't really know what this means, because my beautifully frail-looking and seventy-year-old neighbor, the poet Elsa Gidlow, cultivates a garden which supplies our whole community with vegetables. Come to think of it, what is more mystically and erotically pleasurable than apple trees, rows of lettuce, patches of herbs, vines of runner beans, or plantations of potatoes?

But mankind of the twentieth century is actually feeding on the production of crash and trash—of superweapons, vast slabs of cement, untold miles of wire, and billions of "objects" to be sold in shops which I haven't the slightest wish to own. Almost everyone who works in a city is producing rubbish and symbols of rubbish. This is not to condemn technical skill in the use of fire, metals, electricity, and even computers, but only to ask what on Earth are we doing with it. I repeat the question, WHAT DO WE WANT?

117

I repeat it again and again wherever I go. I have suggested that the college entrance examination be the requirement that every student has to write a detailed paper of his idea of heaven, and that his professor or tutor criticize it for consistency, imagination, and feasibility. I have even suggested to an encounter group that we discuss what might be, here and now, the most delightful forms of relationship between each other, but people seem to want, instead, to worry over their discords.

We do not know what we want because we are only dimly aware of anything wantable. We have taught ourselves to pursue such abstract and weakly perceived goals as happiness, love, goodness, service to others, fun, fame, fortune, power, peace, or God—but we have more words than experience for what we mean.

Therefore I am going to finish off this essay by saying what I myself want, and which, to a satisfactory degree, I already have. I want to spend time sitting still, or walking slowly, wondering at and feeling the basic sense of existence, of being alive-dead, of watching my breath, of hearing all sounds in the air, and of letting clouds and stars caress my eyes. I want to let go of anxiety and turn it into laughter, and realize absolutely that life and death are two sides of the same coin. I want a female companion who will, alternatively, melt into me and wrestle with me, obey me and object to me, admire me and then suddenly show that she can do so many things much better than I. I want to write and talk for interested audiences, to charm them, and play with their questions, but also to listen to people who can tell me things I don't know without being bores. I want to watch water which reflects many changing qualities of light and wind, and is visited by seagulls, pelicans, terns, grebes, and wild duck. I want to sit on some far-out

118

rock or a lonely beach and listen to the waves and look at the Western sky at dawn. I want to shoot arrows so high into the sky that they seem to turn into birds. I want to see mountains and prowl through their foothills and forests, listening, at dusk, to unseen waterfalls.

I want to sit at a typewriter, at certain times, carefully and meticulously putting into words what I feel—the challenge being that it cannot really be put into words at all. I want to go off to a colorful and spacious kitchen to experiment with some new kind of soup or stew, or method of steaming fish, or to see if I can cook with a *wok* (that is, a stir-fry pan) in the manner of the Chinese. Reminding me that I also want to play with the finest Chinese writing brushes and sticks of incensed ink, which you rub into water, and then try out the various ways of dancing on paper which are their form of ideographic writing. I want to be able to allay pain and sickness with the touch of my hands. I want to make a fire of charcoal and burn cedar leaves or sandalwood, late in the evening, while listening or dancing to classical or rock music.

I want to see the reflection of light in glass and crystal, and, lying on the ground, to look up at trees patterning a vivid blue sky. At night to go to sleep beneath them, and to wake just before dawn when the stars can still be seen through their branches. I want to hear the bell of Nanzenji, a temple in Kyoto, at four in the morning—more of a gong than a bell. I want to go to Sikkim and Nepal to see the Himalayas, but not to climb them. I want to enjoy the company of certain friends, to eat Stilton cheese, melons, heavy black bread, and prosciutto, and to drink Gardner's Old Strong, a British ale which is no longer available.

Earthy as it may be, that is a glimpse of my idea of heaven.

I am looking at things so far away
that I'm seeing them as they were
a million years ago, not today.
Out, out beyond our own flat helix of lights
which, by sheer distance, condense as the Milky Way—
    that horizon towards which our planet
    tumbles eastwards all night—
they have only numbers, no names.

But the magician, his voice reverberating
without echo in the dark imaginary dome,
tells me the names of lights nearer home—
names whose strangeness to our tongue
measures the far immensity
of Aldebaran, bright horn of the Bull,
Arcturus, the Plowman's spear,
Betelgeuse and Rigel, the Hunter's jewels,
Vega, playing the Lyre, and Deneb, head of the Swan.

See Rasalhague and Sabik, where the Snake is grasped,
Alphecca in the Northern Crown,
Eltamin, ball for the Dragon,

*Incantation
of the Stars*

Hadar and Menkent, where the Horseman prances,
Fomalhaut with the Fish swimming south,
and Altair, where the Eagle hangs.

We look not up but down into our galaxy,
rolling above a floor of stars
whose center unseen, where the Archer points his arrow,
lies between Shaula and the Shield.
O Algol, Almach, Elnath, and Alpheratz,
Hamal, Mirfak, Antares, and Caph—
with the music of your far-out names
the magician casts a spell upon the sky.

That poem came out of a night spent in the desert, at
Joshua Tree National Monument in southern California,
where the air is so clear that it seems to act as a lens. We
had also a Questar telescope. This was the first time that I
had ever really experienced and understood our relationship to the whole galaxy, and the stars ceased to be merely
a confused display of fireworks over my head. Now I understand why a psychiatrist friend of mine, Dr. Leonard Miller,
uses astronomy for treating his patients.

Earth is in heaven. It spins, falls, and floats in a spiral
nebula. Earth is not opposed to heaven: it belongs in it as
a member of the whole company of the stars. Each of the
three parts of Dante's epic, *The Divine Comedy,* ends with
the word "stars." And anyone who has read Austin Farrer's
commentary on the Apocalypse, *A Rebirth of Images,* will
realize that a preoccupation with astrology and astronomy
underlies the whole notion of heaven as conceived in the
Hebrew, Christian, and Islamic traditions. The authors of

the four Gospels are associated with the four "fixed" signs of the Zodiac: Matthew with Aquarius, Mark with the Lion, Luke with the Bull, and John with the Phoenix-Scorpion, and are often represented thus on the four arms of the Crucifix. What is all this about?

Heaven is always associated with happiness and bliss, as when we say, "It was simply heavenly." Why do the Christians pray to "Our Father, who art in heaven," and believe that Jesus ascended into heaven, and why did the Greeks immortalize their heroes by giving their names to constellations?

We civilized human beings are psychically and sensually myopic. We concentrate on trivial details. We ignore the constant and eternal, and are therefore "ignore-ant" of our real identity as members, functions, expressions, and manifestations of everything that is to be seen in the sky, and much more. We hide ourselves in architectural boxes, fix our attention on scraps of paper, and upon the sundry symbolic noises which we make to each other in representation of things that go on in shops, offices, parlors, and bedrooms.

But when your cat goes out at night, it isn't solely intent on a sexual adventure. It sits and watches the sky; it becomes as familiar with the patterns of the stars as you are with your home-town streets, and therefore can find its way back from (and this has actually been done) Minneapolis to Tucson. The European whitethroat and other birds have also been shown to navigate by the stars on their periodic migrations. Unlike people, they are aware of their cosmic context. They therefore have no need for the quarrelsome artificialities of religions, which substitute words, ideas, and symbols for what can be seen by the naked eye.

How many of us now realize that space is the same thing

as mind, or consciousness? That when you look out into infinity you are looking at yourself? That your inside goes with your entire outside as your front with your back? That this galaxy, and all other galaxies, are just as much you as your heart or your brain? That your coming and going, your waking and sleeping, your birth and your death, are exactly the same kind of rhythmic phenomena as the stars and their surrounding darkness? To be afraid of life is to be afraid of yourself.

Of course, we have tried to organize the stars by giving them places in an imaginary celestial sphere with 360 degrees of latitude, and then, as if the whole sky were a public Rorschach blot, projecting upon them patterned constellations. (I wonder if cats and whitethroats do this.) But I prefer to look at star-patterns as I look at formations of spray and foam, mountains and clouds, marble and smoke. For such things have a peculiar nonsymmetrical *order*—an incalculable order—which the Chinese call *li* and represent with the character 理 which has the original meaning of markings in jade and grain in wood. We recognize instinctively an order in such formations which is quite distinct from the mere chaos of scattered garbage. At the same time it is not an order that is measurable or calculable in terms of our linear systems of words and numbers, which can represent life only in caricature and which, if they could ever be made sufficiently exact to predict the future in full detail, would render that future already known, past, and dead. The order of *li* and of the stars is the order of surprises, of order recognizable as order only because it is playing with randomness.

This is why the enlightenment-wisdom, or *satori*, embodied in Zen Buddhism is said to be:

A direct transmission outside scriptures;
Not dependent on words and letters;
Direct pointing to the heart . . .

that is, to use the most clumsy words, to reality as some no-thing, nonverbal, nonmeasurable, and nonconceptual—where every "non" implies an affirmation rather than a negation, a plus rather than a minus.

And having said *that* I feel like a fool! More and more—perhaps just because I am growing older—it seems to me that the utterances of sociologists, psychologists, and especially philosophers and theologians. are completely meaningless, including also the tart and crusty writings of those who call themselves logical positivists or scientific empiricists. Often they are redeemed by a certain poetic verve or flair of expression which transforms them into music rather than logic, so that one may read such philosophy with the same pleasure as listening to the song of birds just after dawn. Yet most academic philosophers now deride the babblings of mystics and metaphysicians as *mere* poetry, whereas I feel increasingly with R. H. Blyth and Paul Reps that reality *is* poetry.

Thus, as it becomes increasingly mathematical and linear, the science of astronomy dries up into a merely pompous and officious attitude to the stars. So also astrology, as it becomes concerned with predicting the future, becomes entirely insensitive to the actual heavens to such an extent that most astrologers are so preoccupied with ephemeris tables that they hardly look at the stars—just as those who play the stock market are generally unconscious of what the technologies of business are doing to the real and natural world. (They do not realize, for example, that most of the wealth and energy of the United States is being used to

125

employ a huge team of destruction workers to obliterate the flora and fauna of Indochina.)

G. K. Chesterton once said that whereas the philosopher tries to get the heavens into his head, the poet asks only to get his head into the heavens. So when one asks, in today's lingo, "Where's your head at?" it would be ideal to answer that it's in heaven. The problem is that most of us now live in cities where the view of heaven is blocked by ceilings and smog. People don't even realize that every home can be a home with a view—the view of the sky—since we are living on the side of the planet and look not up but out.

This is a way of saying that our deepest spiritual, religious, and psychological problems are extremely simple. Just go out and look at the sky. Get to know where you are. Heaven is there for all to see. It's like the story of the fellow who had chronic "singing in the ears." He went to his family doctor, who could find nothing wrong, and sent him to a otorhinolaryngologist, who could find nothing wrong and sent him to a psychoanalyst, with whom he worked twice a week for a whole year on the symbolism of the ear. But still the singing didn't go away. One day he went to buy some shirts, and when the salesman asked what size he wore he said. "I always take a fourteen." The salesman, who was one of those elderly British-butler types, replied, "Excuse me, sir, but as one used to observing men's necks, I think you should be wearing a fifteen." So the neck was measured, and fifteen it was; and with the new shirts the singing went away.

Now of course I know, in a theoretical way, that the names of most of the stars are Arabic and could be translated into meaningful English words. Happily, I don't understand Arabic, and so the names have magic. Chinese characters on signs in Hong Kong and Tokyo likewise have magic for those who can't read them, and so don't realize that they are merely saying BARBER SHOP or FRESH FISH TODAY. (And of course this isn't so boring if you've only just succeeded in reading Chinese, or if the characters are written with fine calligraphic style.) But what happens when, at an immense cost, we actually get to the moon to find out that, as we actually suspected, it's only a slag heap? That most of the stars are merely radioactive gas-balls surrounded by dead planets? That existence itself is "nothing but" an intensely stupid electronic mechanism? This is like losing one's appetite, or feeling that "all women are the same in the dark." Our technological culture *prides* itself on having no appetite—on discovering that the universe contains neither magic nor mystery, that Mother Nature is just a common slut. Accordingly, therefore, the food actually tastes of plastic, the wine of chemicals, the water of chlorine, and the air of carbon monoxide.

Invariably and inevitably we see nature in our own image. What we think about it is what we think about ourselves, and I suppose one can just as well hate one's neighbor as oneself as love him as oneself. So then: to the degree that you have reduced yourself to a formula, to a specific personality or definable ego, to a miserably sinful creature (with sins all listed for confession), or to a regular psychological type (with dreams all analyzed), you will have put yourself omnipotently in charge of nothing. The trick explained. The magician exposed as a charlatan.

July 1971

A few days ago I gave a ride to a rather pleasant hippie couple who seemed to have no particular destination. I asked, "What trip are you on?" He said, "Like spiritual trip?" I said, "Yes." He said, "We're on the Jesus trip." "Whose Jesus?" I asked, "Billy Graham's or mine?" "Well, it's all sort of the same, isn't it?"

Was Jesus a Freak?

It is not. For Billy Graham follows a long tradition, both Catholic and Protestant, wherein the gospel (or "good news") of Jesus has been eclipsed and perverted by pedestalization, by kicking him upstairs so as to get him out of the way, and by following a religion *about* Jesus instead of the religion *of* Jesus. Obviously, Jesus was not the man he was as a result of making Jesus Christ his personal savior. The religion of Jesus was that he knew he was a son of God, and the phrase "son of" means "of the nature of," so that a son of God is an individual who realizes that he is, and always has been, one with God. "I and the Father are one."

When Jesus spoke those words the crowd took up stones to stone him. He said, "I have shown you many good works from the Father, and for which of them do you stone me?" They answered, "We're not stoning you for a good work but for blasphemy, because you, being a man, make yourself God." And he replied, "Isn't it written in your Law that 'I have said: you are gods'? If he addressed those to whom he gave his words as gods (and you can't contradict the Scriptures), how can you say that I blaspheme because I said 'I am a son of God'?" But the self-styled Christians, and especially the fundamentalist bibliolaters, always insist that Jesus was the *only* son of woman who was also the son of God, and thus call upon all the rest of us to follow the example of the one human freak who had the unique advantage of being the Boss's son. This is not a gospel: it is a chronic hangup, a self-frustrating guilt trip. It isolates the career of Jesus as an exhibit in a glass case—for worship but not for use.

It is obvious to any informed student of the history and psychology of religion that Jesus was one, of many, who had an intense experience of cosmic consciousness—of the vivid realization that oneself is a manifestation of the eternal energy of the universe, the basic "I am." But it is very hard to express this experience when the only religious imagery at your disposal conceives that "I am" as an all-knowing and all-powerful monarch, autocrat, and beneficent tyrant enthroned in a court of adoring subjects. In such a cultural context, you cannot say "I am God" without being accused of subversion, insubordination, megalomania, arrogance, and blasphemy. Yet that was why Jesus was crucified. In India people would have laughed and rejoiced with him, because Hindus know that we are all God in disguise—playing hide-and-seek with himself. Their model of the universe is not based on the political states of the Egyptians, Chaldeans, and Persians, whose awesome dictatorships still hold sway through the Jewish, Christian, and Islamic religions, even in the Republic of the United States. In Hinduism the whole universe is like the Holy Trinity—one as many, and many as one. (And, of course, the Hindus are the despised of the earth, having been reduced to utter poverty by Muslims and Christians.)

But Jesus had to speak through a public-address system —the only one available—which distorted his words, so that they came forth as the bombastic claim to be the one and only appearance of the Christ, of the incarnation of God as man. This is not good news. The good news is that if Jesus could realize his identity with God, you can also— but this God does not have to be idolized as an imperious monarch with a royal court of angels and ministers. God, as "the love which moves the sun and other stars," is something much more inward, intimate, and mysterious—in the sense of being too close to be seen as an object.

So it turns out, alas, that our new breed of Jesus freaks are following the old nongospel of the freaky Jesus—of the bizarre man who was unnaturally born and whose corpse was weirdly reanimated for a space trip into heaven. (One can, of course, interpret these ancient images in a more profound and nonliteral way, as I tried to show in my book *Beyond Theology*.) But to identify Jesus the man as the one and only historical incarnation of a divinity considered as the royal, imperial, and militant Jehovah, is only to reinforce the pestiferous arrogance of "white" Christianity— with all the cruel self-righteousness of its missionary zeal. They may perhaps be forgiven for their ignorance, but today, when we are exposed to all the riches of Earth's varying cultures and religions, there is no further excuse for the parochial fanaticism of spiritual in-groups.

Jesus freaks are still in a state of enthusiastic innocence, as yet unaware of the frightful implications of their claims. But they must realize that Christianity would seem ever so much more valid if it would stop insisting on being an oddity. Christianity has universality, or catholicity, only in recognizing that Jesus is one particular instance and expression of a wisdom which was also, if differently, realized in the Buddha, in Lao-tzu, and in such modern avatars as Ramana Maharshi, Ramakrishna, and, perhaps, Aurobindo and Inayat Khan. (I could make a very long list.) This wisdom is that none of us are brief island existences, but forms and expressions of one and the same eternal "I am" waving in different ways, such that, whenever this is realized to be the case, we wave more harmoniously with other waves.

Christians, who so often affect prickly and astringent attitudes, may cluck and pish-tush that this is all very imprecise, vague, woolly, and sentimental. But in the harsh clacking of their disciplined voices, their accurate distinctions, and precise calculations, I hear the rattle of rifle bolts and the clicking of heels. 'Like a mighty army moves the Church of God." But this is no way for a gentle-man.

September 1, 1970

What are we going to do with an enormous amount of valuable real estate known, not quite correctly, as the Church—whether it be Catholic, Episcopalian, Presbyterian, Lutheran, Methodist, Congregational, or Unitarian? I am going to offer some very practical suggestions, for whereas, on the one hand, "Something is happening and you don't know what it is, do you, Mr. Jones?"—on the other, the theological education of young clergymen has been so vastly improved in recent years that they are baffled by congregations who want everything just as they imagine it always was, even if the pews do get emptier and emptier as they die off.

Talking of pews reminds me that as a child I always thought of church as a bus. The vicar was up front as the driver, and the people sat in long rows observing the backs of each other's necks. The organ music was the sound of the engine. And they were always singing ditties about "Forward!" "Onward!" "Upward!" This kind of church still has some popularity among older people in the more provincial areas of the United

What Shall We Do with the Church?

States. But in the great urban and suburban regions on the two coasts, and about such cities as Chicago, the churches —especially those which have established themselves great cathedrals and "plants"—are in serious financial trouble. For example, it costs some $800 a day just to run the facilities of Grace Cathedral in San Francisco, and about eighty people turn out for the main Sunday service.

I myself was once a clergyman, and was for five years the Episcopal chaplain to students, United States Navy units, and faculty at Northwestern University, so I know whereof I speak from the inside. I am also, and have been for forty years, a student of comparative religion, and have concluded that any form of orthodox, conservative, or fundamentalist Christianity is the most difficult religion in the world to explain to any intelligent person. It can be done, but it takes hours and hours of explaining, and sometimes explaining away, a system of theology, history, and symbolism which is as remote from the comprehension of most educated young people as the religion of the Incas or Aztecs. Some people—like C. S. Lewis, Jacques Maritain, William Temple, and even Dorothy Sayers—have made a good try at it, but one comes away with the feeling that these are such brilliant intellectual types that they could make a good case for any proposition whatsoever—as that the entire solar system is inside the sum (which is easy to argue), or that the entire system of galaxies is the atomic structure in the pimple on the nose of an old lady, who lives a very ordinary life, in an immeasurably larger dimension.

The churches have, for at least a century, been trying to beguile young people into acceptance of this bizarre religion —with negligible results. They have tried young people's fellowships, with dances and pot-luck suppers, drama clubs, discussion groups, sports teams, Bible study circles, choral groups, bingo games, and have even gone so far as to use jazz for their service music and invite rock bands to play at the altar. They have made up prayers and retold Bible stories in hip language. They have opened up crypts and basements as immense pads where vagrant and impoverished hippies can flop for the night. Yet there is the inescapable sensation that all this is bait on a trap—and of course it is, for the Church has been on the make as a missionary organization, counting converts, since its inception, and, with only the most cursory examination of other religions, knows in advance that it is the only really good and true one.

The trap itself is (1) that the Church would persuade you to worship Jesus Christ as your sole Savior and Hero, and to regard him not simply as wise, loving, and divine, but—competitively—as the wisest, most loving, and only truly divine being that has ever walked the earth, and that in some mysterious way, which has never yet been clearly explained, his death by crucifixion paid the price for all our sins, if only we will accept it as having done so. (This is an argument in which the advocate and the judge are invariably the same person or corporation).

(2) The Church will insist that you abstain from all genital sexual activity whatsoever until such time as you are monogamously wedded, preferably under the Church's auspices. Under the present economic and educational system this should keep most lusty people completely frustrated until at least twenty-three, unless parents are willing to help out, and then again it is extremely foolhardy to embark upon a monogamous marriage until you are at least forty.

135

(3) When you become a member, the Church will expect of you an annual pledge of *x* dollars, to be divided between missionary work and the maintenance of your own particular church, and which goes chiefly for utilities, paying the minister's salary, and, above all, paying off the mortgage on a whopping Gothic-style building.

(4) The Church will expect you to attend at least one of its services regularly, every Sunday, and with very, very few exceptions these are universally abominable. In the first place they consist almost exclusively of talk. We tell God what to do and what not to do, and give him information about things which, if he is omniscient, he already knows. We attempt to celebrate his glory with doggerels and religious nursery rhymes called hymns, mostly set to military or sentimental tunes. And then the minister, speaking on God's behalf, thinks up ear-catching ways of spinning out platitudes concerning the avoidance of evil and the cultivation of goodness. The Roman Catholic Church recently made the serious mistake of having the Mass celebrated everywhere in the vernacular, so that it could be "understood," and added insult to injury by having some person standing with a microphone beside the altar to "explain" what was going on, thereby depriving Christendom of the last widespread stronghold of mystery. To find it any more you have to go to such joyous places as the Russian Orthodox Cathedral in Paris, where there are no pews, and the rite is celebrated in Old Slavonic, which nobody understands. It was the same with the medieval Latin of the Roman Church. Even if you knew Latin quite well, it was so chanted or mumbled as to be perfectly unintelligible.

Why should a religious service be unintelligible? Because its function is, to quote Keats, "to tease us out of thought, as doth eternity." For many people the contemplation of God, of the Ground of Being, is most easily reached through the contemplation of pure sound, which is why Hindus and Buddhists hum very slowly such virtually meaningless mantras as OM AH HUM. Christians could just as well use AMEN, IESUS, ADONAI, ALLELUIA, or KYRIE ELEISON. To contemplate through sound in this way, you must simply be absorbed in the sound itself and forget all about anything it is supposed to mean, for when words are used for their meaning they become abstract signs and symbols, pointing to something other than themselves, and one step removed from reality. Services therefore should be focused on meditation and contemplation, still using chanting and appropriate music, though I feel the organ has such maudlin associations attached to it that it has had its day.

The next step is to strip the churches of pews, leaving only a few chairs around the walls for old people and invalids, and otherwise cover the floors with carpets and cushions. Ministers should not be required to wear two sets of clothes, with their vestments covering their ordinary street clothes or cassocks, but should wear white or colored robes with hoods, like the Greek chlamys. And none should preach a sermon longer than ten minutes. And none should be asked to go about in that supreme symbol of stuffiness and self-righteousness, the uncomfortable round starched collar. There is no reason why Mass should not be celebrated in such churches, but rather for the mood and attitude of worship than for the didactic meaning of what is said—using Latin, Greek, Old Slavonic, Sanskrit, or Hebrew. I have myself made up a Mass called the *Missa Glossolalia* or the Mass of the Gift of Tongues. I go through the whole traditional action of the Mass, but what I should

137

chant, in any language or no language, I leave to the Spirit and thus need no book beside me.

The next reforms may be harder for conservative church people to take. I think we should abandon petitionary prayers. We might focus the psychic energy of the congregation upon given individuals in trouble. But if God is loving, omnipotent, and omniscient, to attempt to draw his attention to a sick friend or relative is sheer impertinence and even lack of faith—for if such a God exists he is taking much better care of your Aunt Susan with cancer than either you or her doctors. In my own theology Aunt Susan is, like everyone else, God in disguise, playing hide-and-seek with himself at an extreme end of the spectrum of "hide," at which extreme point Aunt Susan may well do a flip and discover who and what she really is. For Christian theologians have not yet discovered that the spirit, or *pneuma,* in man, far superior to the soul, psyche, or *nephesh,* is none other than the *ruach Adonai,* the one and indivisible divine energy itself. One must assume that such a person as Jesus lived consciously and continuously from the *ruach Adonai,* and not from the *nephesh,* or ego. It is thus said by Quoheleth, the preacher of the book of Ecclesiastes, that at death the body shall return to the dust, and the Spirit to God who gave it. In any case, prayers for this, that, and the other put God at a distance, when even a great theologian has said that God is nearer to you than you are to yourself. They likewise distract attention from the many ways of meditation or contemplation which introduce us to mystical experience, or immediate realization of our union with God. The substitution of interminable chatter for this realization is the basic reason why the Church has no spiritual power, except among some few silent monks like Trappists and Carthusians, and even their power is wobbly because they deny themselves the spiritual and physical regeneration of sexual communion.

There is another necessary reform which the die-hards may find even more difficult to take, which is that the Church must abandon its spiritual imperialism and its craze for making converts. It must desist from its proud and arbitrary claim to be top religion, and from the impertinence of sending missionaries to persuade so-called heathens to substitute Christianity for religions of which such missionaries know next to nothing. Missionaries did much to ruin the cultures of Hawaii and Polynesia; their work lies close to the roots of the barbarous apartheid system of South Africa; they successfully destroyed Inca, Mayan, and Aztec culture; they founded those very colleges in China where most of the leaders of the Communist Revolution received their training. Under the dispensation of Lord Macaulay they nearly succeeded in obliterating the culture of India. With the exception of some strictly medical missionaries, missionaries as a whole have wrought incalculable harm, and have nowhere succeeded in bringing all mankind to the feet of Christ. One must say to the Church, "Put up or shut up."

The Church has much to learn from so-called heathens. A Benedictine monk has recently written on Christian Yoga, and another, as well as a Jesuit, has written on Christian Zen. They have a lot to teach us about splendid meditative rituals, and about joyous religious dancing—for lack of which many of our churches feel like grim courts of law where we are all on trial for unspecified crimes, and where the Judge has to be wheedled and flattered most humbly into showing mercy. Nevertheless, the Church still comprises individuals of high intelligence and good-will, and is still legal owner and controller of a formidable amount of property—churches, halls, schools, and retreat houses. I am willing to bet that if the reforms I am suggesting were adopted, if all anxiety about every-member canvasses were forgotten, if ministers would let slip the folly of making formal parish calls, and if moralistic preachments were indefinitely suspended, the churches would suddenly be thronged by thousands of young people, who might even be willing to pay a reasonable admission fee at the door—attracted there, not by a dismal sense of duty, but by the one thing the Church should be offering and is not: spiritual and mystical experience.

For reasons still unclear to me, most clergymen are afraid of this dimension of the spiritual life. They say it leads to private and personal religious whimsies which need always to be checked against standards of sound doctrine and the traditions of the universal Church. It does not seem to strike them that the very acceptance of such standards is a matter of personal whimsy and opinion. They are like the Bandar-Log, the monkeys, in Kipling's *Jungle Book* who used to get together and scream, "We all say so, so it *must* be true!" It has always seemed to me that when you come into contact with a large group of people who share a common belief—say, in numerology, or in flying saucers as visitors from outer space, the consensus is apt to overwhelm your own good judgment.

The practical problem is therefore to find sufficient clergy with the ability and the attitude to conduct services in the manner which I have very briefly described, and to let many of those more bizarre features of Christianity go by default because they are never satisfactorily explained except by endless talk—the inheritance of Original Sin from Adam, the Immaculate Conception of Mary, the Virgin Birth of Jesus, the Atonement for sin by his crucifixion, his physical resurrection from death, his corporeal Ascension into Heaven, and the resurrection of our own bodies from death on the morning of the Last Judgment, which will consign us both physically and spiritually to everlasting bliss or to everlasting torture. Interesting as these archetypes may be to the student of mythology, there is no way of proving conclusively that they are untrue, nor would those who hold them to be true be able to imagine any evidence which would show the contrary. They are simply implausible. They do not speak to our condition, and are meaningless in our universe of discourse. They are not even of interest to anyone following the contemplative, mystical way—at least, not in this day and age. There is no point in attacking them; just let them slide away.

I believe there are many clergy of almost all denominations, except the Protestant lunatic fringe, who would be happy and eager to give a lead in this new-old kind of religion—to get away from "Jesus Loves Me, This I Know," and from spending hours trying to prepare interesting sermons about small points. A relatively short period of training could give them the necessary ability, and they would learn the rest as they went along, but they would end up with a real religion instead of a talk-and-sing-fest, at which everyone dons his most uncomfortable clothes, and maintains a demure, stand-offish attitude to everyone else, and is shown to his pew by an usher with a white carnation in his buttonhole. Of course, there is a good argument for just letting obsolete institutions fall apart, since "no man putteth new wine into old wineskins," and let them be replaced by such new institutions as the growth centers. I may be presumptuous, but I think I can show the churches a workable solution.

141

September 10, 1970

The question seems impolite, and yet it is no more so than asking, Do you see? Do you hear? Do you feel? Do you taste? We admire a person of taste, but what is wrong with a person of smell? The problem is superficially one of bad usage in English grammar. "To smell" should mean to sense through the nose, and "a smell" should mean no more than a nasal sensation. A person with an offensive body odor should be said "to stink," and an unpleasant nasal sensation should be called "a stink" or "a stench," never "a smell," for the term is as neutral as "a sound." We have some nouns for pleasant smells—a fragrance, a perfume, an aroma. But I can find no verb which is the antonym of "to stink," and which means to give forth or to detect a pleasant smell, like the Japanese *kaori*. Furthermore, we have very few adjectives which apply specifically to the sense of smell—pungent, acrid, fragrant, putrid, aromatic. "Smelly" and "stinky" are simply verbal adjectives. "Odoriferous" is simply an affected Latinism for "smelly," while "musky," "grassy," "fishy," and "leathery" say no

Do You Smell?

143

more than, for example, the smell of the musk flower. I would like, for example, to introduce the word "chuffly," to denote all those qualities of smell having a dusty or chalky texture—blackboard chalk, face powder, smoke, street dust, and so on.

But we have no spectrum of smell, such as we have of light, nor scales and *ragas*, such as we have of sound, A cat may look at a king, and I may listen with obvious attentiveness to what you are saying. I may sip your wine with overt gusto, and may even grasp your hand on meeting. It is even now becoming customary among young men in America to embrace each other. But quite deliberately to sniff another person, unless she is your sweetheart, is beyond the pale and puts us in mind of dogs, snuffling at each other's bottoms. Aside from perfume on a woman or after-shave lotion on a man, you are not supposed to be smelly at all, though we also make exceptions for such disinfectant smells as are given off by Lavoris, Listerine, and Binaca. Yet a skillful *parfumier* will study a woman's body odor with great care, considering just what other ingredients will transform it into a unique perfume. But on the whole, most of us prefer each other to be odoriferously anonymous. Some of us like roses, hyacinths, or potpourri in our homes, but on the whole houses and offices are supposed to be odorless. As G. K. Chesterton put it—

> They haven't got no noses,
> And goodness only knowses
> The noselessness of man.

What this really means is that smell is a repressed sense. It exists all the time, but is ritually ignored, as certain types of scientists will ritually ignore hunches and other parapsychological perceptions. Freud was, I think, correct in showing us that repressed energies become amazingly powerful but not necessarily in constructive ways. Thus, as is well known, we habitually ignore and fail to have conscious memory of much that has been right before our eyes or spoken loud and clearly into our ears. I knew an archbishop with a superb voice, but can't remember a single thing he said, and have had long conversations with women without the vaguest recollection of how they were dressed.

But when an entire sense is virtually repressed it becomes unconsciously powerful—the sense of "the unconscious"—and it is thus that through smell we form apparently irrational likes and dislikes for other people and places. The power of smell is also recognized by the uncanny way in which it can evoke vivid memories and moods. We imagine that through liberal use of soap and water, decent Caucasian people do not emit any unpleasant odor. But wash as he may, a meat eater stinks in the nostrils of a vegetarian, and the odor of a well-soaped Englishman is a stench to a Hottentot who, *per contra*, enjoys the company of his own people, who comb their hair with rancid butter. Now it *is* true that people of quality carried nosegays, or bunches of well-scented flowers, in those ancient cities of Europe which had open drains oozing along the gutters of the streets. Things were somewhat better in Japan, where human excrements were towed away in "honey-carts" to be dumped into pits on the farms and spread on the fields when mature.

We cannot, therefore, be too sure of the common Protestant idea that incense was used at religious ceremonies to counteract the collective stink of unwashed crowds. It was discovered that certain odors had powerful effects upon

145

mood—that incense made from pine, cedar, or aloeswood reminded one of high, lonely forests, of environments particularly conducive to quiet contemplation. Sandalwood, the most common basis for incense in Asia, is slightly more erotic, yet undoubtedly woodsy—suggesting the forests of the tropics rather than the mountains. Other substances are used—musk, jasmine, rose, wildwood, and mogra flowers, but these on the whole are more suitable for the boudoir than the temple. The temple incense of the Middle East and the West is basically frankincense, which is an aromatic gum resin collected from a variety of Asian and African trees of the genus *Boswellia*. It is the characteristic odor of a Roman Catholic church. Beware of any incense in stick, cube, or cone form colored black or dark purple, for these are apt to have the cloying odor of bad, sultry perfume mixed with soap. It is not simply that *all* black or dark purple incenses are of this noxious type, for some of the very best are of these colors. So far as I know no good incense is made in this country, other than the beige cones of juniper and pine that are made in New Mexico and Vermont. Insist on trying samples before you buy, and remember that a good incense should, when burning, somewhat resemble its odor before lighting.

Incense usually comes in two forms—stick, or powder or granules. Occasionally sandalwood may be had in chips. The stick has several functions: it is self-burning, the point of light on the tip is often used for concentration in yoga, and the burning down of the stick measures the time—especially for a period of meditation. Powdered, granular, or chip incense is usually burned on charcoal, using either ordinary briquettes, or better, a special type of disk, self-lighting charcoal impregnated with saltpeter which can be purchased at any shop selling Roman Catholic church goods, or any *bondieuserie.* Catholics, both Western and Eastern Orthodox, usually light this charcoal in the bottom of thuribles, which are brass or silver pots with perforated lids, and suspended from chains. These are ceremoniously swung by the clergy at the altar or at the people, and are tended by a special acolyte known as the thurifer. The thurible of Hindus and Buddhists is a similar brass pot with perforated lid, but it has a wooden handle, like a saucepan, instead of chains. Otherwise Buddhists use various forms of *koro,* which are simply vessels of bronze, cloisonné, brass, or ceramic, filled with a mixture of sand and ash as a base for either sticks or charcoal. I have even seen a self-burning incense laid out upon smooth sand in a wide *koro* in a continuous arabesque of lines that formed an esoteric Buddhist symbol. This was at Jodo-in, a temple on Mount Hiei, above Kyoto, which is so ancient, remote, and peaceful that I have called it "the shrine at the end of the world."

Normally Zen Buddhists use *jinko,* or aloeswood—a diseased part of the tree which becomes hard and nubbly in form, and is relatively expensive. It is best to burn it, not directly on the charcoal, but on a sliver of foil or a small ceramic dish about the size of a quarter. The Chinese and Indochinese make a very agreeable "punk" incense which fends off insects and has an odor reminiscent of burning piles of fallen leaves on an autumn afternoon. It comes in long, thick brown sticks or in green coils. Amerindians like to use the actual leaves of cedar or juniper, throwing them upon the hot embers of a ceremonial fire such as is used at the peyote ceremony, where the Road Man, or leader, has the Cedar Man sitting at his left to keep the teepee incensed all night.

147

Now, no one can assert that incense, except the few types against which I have warned you, stinks. Why, then, do not Protestants burn it at their religious ceremonies, nor most people have it in their homes? Catholics refer to people who avoid incense as having "Protestant noses." Is it a waste of money? No more so than stained-glass windows, choir surplices, preachers' gowns, organs, lecterns, pulpits, and altar flowers. Is it against the Bible? The Old Testament is full of directions for the proper use of incense, warning only that it should not be used as a substitute for true worship. Is it reminiscent of popery? No more so than surplices, than kneeling to pray, than a cross and even two candlesticks on the altar, nor than the outrageous popery of the Episcopal Church, where the two principal Sunday services are usually the monastic offices of matins and vespers, as distinct from the Eucharist. Is burning it in your home a secret sign that you are a homosexual? Try that one out on me!

The first reason, which I have already mentioned, is that we suppress the sense of smell in general, perhaps in preparation for living in atmospheres where we hardly dare breathe. The second is that it is allegedly foreign to the culture—like eating seaweed, raw fish, snails, broiled eels, octopus, water chestnuts, lotus roots, bamboo shoots, and seagull eggs—thus leaving us blisslessly ignorant of the delights we are missing.

But the third goes deeper still. With the support of incense both religion and sex can "get under your skin" and reach that nonverbal and ecstatic level at which one is tempted to let go and abandon oneself, and such Christians and Jews who believe more firmly in the Devil than in God are always afraid that if they let go, the Devil will take over first, unaware that *not* having let go *is* the Devil already in full control. For ordinary self-control is the domination of one's behavior by the selfish self: its love is assumed, pretensive, and dutiful; its righteousness is hypocritical; its chastity issues in cruelty; its spiritual ideals are highbrow ways of inflating the ego; its profuse confessions of sin are subtle ways of one-upping more ordinary people; and its beneficence has an odd way of arousing resentment in its recipients.

For years I have tried to temper this humorless and inhumane selfish self-denial, this closed and clothes-pegged nose attitude to life, and to reform its ingenious but destructive technologies with the more relaxed, humorous, and pleasurable spirituality of Asia. Incense and its general use are but one aspect of the approach.

April 10, 1968

You yourself are the eternal energy which appears as
this universe. You didn't come into this world. You
came out of it, like a wave from the ocean. You are
not a stranger here. On the contrary, everything that
happens to you, everything that you experience, is
your karma: your own doing. This, though expressed
in differing ways, is the central philosophy of both
Hinduism and Buddhism, cradled alike in the culture
of ancient India.

Obviously, this "you yourself" is not the superficial
personality or ego that we know as John or Jane Doe,
which does not feel itself directly responsible for growing hair or beating a heart, much less for blowing the
wind or shining the stars. The Hindu and Buddhist
sadhanas (or spiritual disciplines) are ways of awak-
ening to the actual sensation of oneself as a process
vaster by far than what is ordinarily felt to be "I"—
that very limited center of conscious attention and
volition which we call the person or ego.

As in watching anything intently—such as the
form of a beautiful woman—one's attention becomes

151

fastened upon particular details, so the basic energy of this universe becomes fascinated with particular plots and patterns, and thus identifies itself with each and every "I"— whether human, animal, or vegetable. But in each instance of doing this, it temporarily forgets that it is *what* there is, *all* that there is, the "which than which there is no whicher" for ever and ever.

Thus every individual is, as it were, God in disguise, playing hide-and-seek with himself through the ages of eternity. "God" is not, in this Hindu view, the universal monarch and governor of Jewish and Christian theology, but rather the Player and Actor of the world, playing all the parts of life so rapidly and intensely that he forgets himself and becomes identified with each one of them. Every role he assumes is also audience to all the others, and the play is performed so convincingly that the audience takes it "for real."

According to Indian philosophy, there are two principal ways by which you may become free from this fascination and so remember your original identity as the source and ground of the universe.

The first and better known is by renunciation of pleasure, by detachment and asceticism, as a means of breaking fascination with the particular forms of life. The self-tormented fakir on his bed of nails is trying to attain to a state in which nothing—but nothing—in life can throw him. He returns to center by plumbing the sensation of pain to its depths, attaining final freedom from the fear of suffering and death.

The second, less known, way—called Tantra—is the opposite: not withdrawal from life but the fullest possible acceptance of one's desires, feelings, and situation as a human being. If you are the Godhead, the universal self, fascinated with the particular existence of John Doe, then just *be* that and *do* that to the full. Explore the fascination of desire, love, and lust to its limit. Accept and enjoy without reservation the ego that you seem to be.

Thus, the follower of the Tantric way plunges himself into just those things which the ascetic renounces: sexuality, food and drink, and all the involvements of worldly life. He does not, however, do this in the half-hearted and timid spirit of the ordinary pleasure seeker. He abandons himself to the pleasure-pain of ordinary sensual experience with the utmost concentration on the finest vibrations of feeling, and learns to play these sensations as one plays with the breath on a flute.

Through this intense exploration of sensory experience he discovers two things. First, that existence or energy is at root a simple alternation or vibration of on and off, yes and no, now you see it/now you don't, which is capable of infinite complication, as all numbers can be represented with the symbols 0 and 1. He learns that the "yes" or "on" element of energy cannot be experienced without contrast with the "no" or "off," and therefore that darkness and death are by no means the mere absence of light and life, but rather their origin. In this way the fear of death and nothingness is entirely overcome.

Because of this startling discovery, so alien to our normal common sense, he worships the divinity under its female rather than its male form—for the female is symbolically representative of the negative, dark, and hollow aspect of the world, without which the masculine, positive, light, and solid aspect cannot be manifested or seen. The very word "Tantra" is connected with the art of weaving, and denotes the interdependence of warp and woof in woven cloth: the one cannot hold together without the other.

153

Second, he discovers that existence is basically a kind of dancing or music—an immensely complex energy pattern which needs no explanation other than itself—just as we do not ask what is the *meaning* of fugues by Bach or sonatas by Mozart. We do not dance to reach a certain point on the floor, but simply to dance. Energy itself, as William Blake said, is eternal delight—and all life is to be lived in the spirit of rapt absorption in an arabesque of rhythms.

Tantric imagery in painting, sculpture, and ritual has, therefore, particular themes which exemplify its own way of experiencing the world. It shows the male and female divinities joined in a meditative form of sexual union in which each worships the other as his and her origin. It shows the god or goddess as a many-headed or multi-armed being, a sort of cosmic centipede, portraying every individual as a limb of the central and eternal self. It also employs patterns of meaningless letters and chants of meaningless sounds (mantras) to suggest and help one to realize the essentially musical and dancing spirit of the universe.

Some understanding of Tantra is therefore a marvelous and welcome corrective to certain excesses of Western civilization. We overaccentuate the positive, think of the negative as "bad," and thus live in a frantic terror of death and extinction which renders us incapable of "playing" life with an air of noble and joyous detachment. Failing to understand the musical quality of nature, which fulfills itself in an eternal present, we live for a tomorrow which never comes—like an orchestra racing to attain the finale of a symphony. But through understanding the creative power of the female, of the negative, of empty space, and of death, we may at least become completely alive in the present.

April 1972

The individual is an aperture through which the whole energy of the universe is aware of itself, a vortex of vibrations in which it realizes itself as man or beast, flower or star—not alone, but as central to all that surrounds it. These centers are not, as it may seem, apart from their surroundings, but stand in mutual relationship to them—center to circumference—in the same way as the magnetic poles. It is, thus that each center anywhere implies all other centers elsewhere. The individual is not, therefore, only a center. He is the entire surround centered at this time or this place, which is why the astrologers try to infer the character of an individual from the disposition of the universe encircling him, though it is doubtful whether they know how to read it correctly.

The whole system is symbiotic in principle, for no individual can appear, for however short a time, except in mutual interdependence with the whole. For it could be said, in the rather clumsy language of nouns and verbs which arbitrarily distinguishes things

The Art of Contemplation

This essay has already been published in the form of a reproduction of the original handwritten manuscript (Society for Comparative Philosophy, 1972, and Pantheon Books, 1973). It is included here for convenience, in a more compact and—possibly—legible form.

from events, that the individual is something which the whole is doing, and that the whole is something which the individual is doing simultaneously. This relationship is not ordinarily felt or recognized in human consciousness, fascinated as it is by the apparent independence of the individual from the whole—and also frightened by it. The individual feels restricted to the area of his voluntary behavior, since all else seems to be an independent and uncontrollable happening on the part of something quite other than himself. He does not realize that, just as one cannot walk without ground, one cannot experience doing except in relation to happening, or self (center) except in relation to other (surround). Thus nothing other than oneself is *quite* other, for between self and other, doing and happening, there is, again, the same kind of unity which exists between magnetic poles, or between the crest and the trough of a wave.

The system as a whole appears to be a distribution of solid entities or modes of energy in the midst of emptiness or space. Human consciousness preoccupies itself with these entities and virtually ignores their spatial background. We consider it "nothing" in the sense of that which has neither importance nor significance, forgetting that without the spatial field none of these entities could be manifested or distinguished. There is, however, between space and entity the same polar relationship as between crest and trough, for which reason nothingness is not simply the contrary or absence of being but rather its ground and origin. We believe so firmly in the maxim *"ex nihilo nihil fit"*— nothing can come out of nothing—that it is almost impossible for us to see that emptiness is the essential prerequi-

156

site for every form of being, unless we can conceive that space has some structure concealed from our senses.

While there are indeed such structures or processes as cosmic rays which do not appear to the naked senses, the usefulness and potency of emptiness is, as Lao-tzu said, precisely that it is perfectly empty. "Being and nonbeing arise mutually." Thus not to see the unity of self and other is the fear of life, and not to see the unity of being and nonbeing is the fear of death.

To understand the reciprocity or mutual interdependence of polar opposites—being and nothing, center and surround, self and other, doing and happening—might be called polar vision. I have been speaking of it in the dry terms of logic, through which it may be grasped intellectually. But when polar vision comes in the form of immediate sensation and feeling, it is known as mystical experience or cosmic consciousness, and of this it is better to speak in the mode of poetry and paradox. Thus, to feel polar vision is to feel that what happens to you is your own doing, and that your own doing is happening to you; that death and emptiness are the firm ground upon which life walks; and that oneself, as both center and surround, is the eternal universe. But this feeling, or intuition, does not come in the form of words or ideas and does not depend on any trick of imagination or self-suggestion. It is more as when one simply sees blue sky or feels that one is alive.

This feeling, or rather, the basis for it, is always present. We are unaware of it only because our consciousness is distracted by another and incompatible feeling of identity which almost all thinking peoples learn from childhood. All too easily, we confuse symbols and signs with what they represent, as in saying, "This *is* a tree," when that to which we are pointing is quite other than the sound "tree." At a much deeper level we confuse what we actually are, as center-and-surround or organism-and-environment, with an idea, concept, or image of ourselves from which the inter-dependence of self and other is absent. This image we call the "I," the ego, the person, or the subject (as distinct from the object). We consider it as the doer of our deeds, the thinker of our thoughts, and the feeler of our feelings. It is a false image for three reasons.

The first is that it is only a concept or symbol and thus can no more do anything than the word "water" can quench thirst. The second is that it is no more than an impoverished caricature of our whole organism, since there is nothing in it which corresponds to the subconscious processes of our being. The third is that it entirely leaves out the polar unity of the organism with the universe, ignoring the fact that the two are a single process.

Under the impression that this pure abstraction is the vital core and organizing center of our being, we try to exert its "will" when action is difficult or emotions hard to restrain. Thus in "taking a hard look" at something, or listening intently, we tighten muscles in the regions of the eyes and ears. We scratch our heads when we are puzzled and frown when we are trying to pay close attention. We grit our teeth when trying to endure pain, clench our fists when trying to "hold on to ourselves," and tighten our stomach muscles when attempting to restrain anxiety. All these actions are futile and do nothing to attain the desired objectives. But they are chronic and habitual and build up a generalized state of bodily tension, often centered just above and between the eyes, which serves as the referent, the felt experience, corresponding to the symbol-image of the person or ego—thus marrying an illusion to a futility.

The question, "What, then, can be done to overcome this false sense of identity and to replace it with polar vision and cosmic consciousness?" is impossible to answer in its own terms. All that needs to be experienced for cosmic consciousness is already present, and anything in excess of this would be obstructive and redundant—like red ink on a rose. Otherwise, it is simply necessary to see that our usual "I" is a false and impotent image. But just as this phantom cannot actually will or do anything, it cannot get rid of itself. No tensing of muscles or, for that matter, deliberate relaxing of muscles, no repetitions of formulae, no self-suggestion, no exercises of imagination, no psychophysical regimens of any kind, will do anything but add strength to the phantom. For every littlest movement to change, or to try not to change, the way you actually feel now will be just one more of those futile muscular tensions (like trying to lift an airliner off the ground by straining at your seatbelt) which give semblance to the reality of the separated ego. You, considered as that ego, cannot get polar vision or cosmic consciousness. It might arise all of itself, as if by divine grace, but there is nothing, just nothing, you can do or not do to bring it about. Yogis and Zen followers sometimes come to this point after long and heroic efforts.

At this point there is nothing to do except what is happening of itself. All that remains is the simple awareness of what is going on—trees outside, street sounds, clock ticking, sunlight on carpet, breathing, body feelings, talking to yourself in your head. Usual cosmic jazz. That's what there is, and every bit of it, including memories and recollections, is happening now. It comes out of nothing as sounds come

159

out of silence, for it should be obvious that the universe has always started from now and left traces behind, like a pen as it writes, though the written record, the seeming past, is still and only now.

You, as ego, cannot change what you are feeling, and you cannot, effectively, try not to change it. There is simply and only what is happening, including those particular thoughts, images, and tensions which you customarily attributed to the phantom thinker and doer. They persist like echoes, but as it is seen that they are just static in the nervous system and not the work of any central ego, they lose interest, subside, and go away of themselves. Hoping that they will go away is just more static.

If you have understood all this, you are simply aware of what is happening now, and we might call this state meditation or, better, contemplation. But it is not that *you* are something which is just watching what happens. "What happens" is just using your organism to watch itself. It is the universe centering as a particular being, though it is not necessary to use or insist on this concept, for what is important here is not the idea but the feeling of it. The words are only a special use of noises in the air, marks on paper, or vibrations in the brain.

If this becomes clear, the effort to transform one's own mind should collapse, and along with it the whole illusion that one is a separate center of consciousness to which experience happens and for which these happenings are problematic. This collapse would then become the state of contemplation, the realization that all is One. I may understand this point theoretically, but still there seems to be no change, for which reason I look for some process whereby I can move from theoretical to immediate or intuitive understanding—not recognizing that this is still a subtle form of the absurd attempt to transform the transformer, arising from the illusory distinction of thinker and thought, experiencer and experience.

So long as this subtle confusion remains, one can be beguiled into various ways of trying to meditate, and a competent guru will suggest techniques so clever that their absurdity will be difficult to discover without resolute attempts to follow them through. Furthermore, the aspirations and minor successes of other seekers will compound a collective illusion, and even a mutual one-upmanship contest, of believing that this or that method or guru is, at last, the one that really works. Yet the intention of the guru himself is simply to exhaust the energy of the illusion by bringing his disciples again and again to experiences of the absurdity of trying to transform mind with mind. As the Zen patriarch Seng-ts'an put it:

> The wise person does not strive;
> The ignorant man ties himself up . . .
> If you work on your mind with your mind,
> How can you avoid an immense confusion?

But once it has been explained, you may naturally ask whether it is really necessary to go through all this rigorous folly to dissipate the illusion. You will wonder whether knowing in advance, theoretically, that these disciplines are absurd, you will no longer have the motivation to follow them through. Yet shouldn't it be clear that the very question "Is it necessary in order to dissipate?" arises directly from the illusion itself? If it isn't clear, you will have the itch to go through the discipline and try to "get"

some attainment and rise to some higher rank of spirituality. But if it is clear, you may feel completely nonplussed
and confounded, as if—as they say in Zen—you were a
mosquito trying to bite an iron bull. However, this feeling
is precisely the sensation that there is no separate self which
can either do or not do anything about the problem. Thus
it may appear, further, that if there is no distinct ego to be
nonplussed, the stream of experience can simply flow on
unobstructed by itself. Hence the verse:

> Blue mountains are of themselves blue mountains;
> White clouds are of themselves white clouds.

This unobstructed flow is the Tao, the way or course of
nature, and is also what is meant by the state of nonattach-
ment—a spontaneous, unforced and unblocked flowing of
life. Yet the prospect of such flowing as a way of life gives
us intense moral anxiety, for at once there are qualms about
unleashing the tigers and demons within us if no control is
exercised. But such qualms are, again, symptoms of the
same old illusion. What if there has been no controlling
self all along? Consider, too, whether the human condition
could be much more depraved than it is already, and mark
the horrendous behavior of people who believe in will
power and in control over their minds and their circumstances. Hitler was an ascetic; Rasputin had incredible
mastery of his mind and body; and many of the samurai
exploited Zen training for the improvement of military
skills, though there were a few, like Miyamoto Musashi,
who finally realized the futility of the enterprise. The Tao
flows without obstruction whether we know it or not, for
the not-knowing is no more than a variant pattern of the
flow. As another Zen verse puts it:

If you understand, things are just as they are;
If you do not understand, things are just as they are.

Now, it is widely believed that those who are free from the illusion of separateness are automatically endowed with extraordinary powers, and this is true in the obvious sense that all the wonders of nature are no other than oneself. Beyond this, the gifts of psionic powers (*siddhi*) may or may not be manifested, just as there may or may not be good weather. In any milieu where the liberated guru is highly revered, people will faith-heal themselves of sickness in his presence and attribute the cure to his magic. But meditation may be regarded as a state in which the fruits of nature and the potentialities of the human organism may develop more richly, though this will never happen if their growth is forced. So long, then, as we are concerned with powers, we are still aiming at increased control of nature and aggravating our frustrations. I am speaking, needless to say, of a control of nature supposedly imposed from the outside. It is really incorrect to think of nature as controlled, self-controlled, or uncontrolled, for the idea of control always involves a duality in which one element commands and the other obeys, or refuses to obey. The pattern or order of nature depends on no such division, since cause and effect, action and reaction, are simply two aspects or poles of a single process, or two ways of looking at it. No cause is separate from its effect, except for purposes of description in a dualistic language.

As a rule, the mystics and gurus who are no longer seeking any attainment go on with what appear to be the formal practices of meditation. The various Buddhas and Bodhisattvas are usually depicted in the position of meditating in

163

the *padmasana*, or lotus posture, like any novice, but this is actually a ritual which is done for its own sake—as one might play the flute, or dance, or invite friends to a formal dinner. It is almost ridiculous to ask, "Why meditate?" as if it were going out of one's way to do something bizarre, like lying on a bed of nails. Why look at the stars or watch clouds? Why go sailing to no fixed destination? Nothing is really explained by its cause or motivation, for we find only causes behind causes until we can pursue them no longer. It is like a child asking, "Why? why? why?" until its father, like a Zen master, says, "O shut up and suck your lollipop!"

Thus contemplation as a particular "exercise," done in a formal way, is simply the ritual enjoyment of that basic awareness of what is happening now which goes on always from moment to moment. In the same way, dancing as dancing is the ritual form of dancing while cooking, or dancing with the pen while writing. It is therefore quite against the spirit of such contemplation to undertake it in a mood of grim seriousness, as is sometimes the way in monasteries and religious communities which are really schools for adolescents without true vocation to the contemplative life, where young people are drilled in ritual like conscripted soldiers. Children should under no circumstances be forced to participate in such exercises, just as we would not dream of requiring them to engage in sexual intercourse. In such ritual it is equally absurd to treat ourselves as children and to browbeat ourselves into arduous practice with the thought that it will be good for us. The good of contemplation is contemplation—not some result that it may bring.

While there are traditional forms of the contemplative ritual, there are no fixed ways in which it must be done. It has, however, been found appropriate to sit like a Buddha with the legs crossed, or in lotus posture, with the back easily erect and the breath coming and going on its own—as if it were falling out and falling in, not as being pushed out or pulled in.

In the same spirit, one does not listen, but simply hears all sounds that are emerging from silence without making any effort to place or identify them. Similarly, one does not look, but only sees light, color, and form playing with the eyes as they, too, emerge moment by moment from the void. Thoughts, likewise, are treated in the same way as sounds, and, if they arise, are merely watched without comment as they come and go; one "hears" them in the same way one would hear the chattering of birds on the roof.

When the breath subsides into a slow rhythm, it is a special delight to let the voice float a tone upon it, with the sound OM, or the mantram OM AH HUM, and to hear the tone reverberating—perhaps to the accompaniment of a gong which is allowed to hum until its sound fades into all other sounds. There are many suitable forms of such chanting ritual, employing not only prolonged single tones, but also rhythmic phrases repeated again and again, as for instance the familiar lilting mantram HARI KRISHNA, HARI KRISHNA, KRISHNA KRISHNA, HARI HARI; HARI RAMA, HARI RAMA, RAMA RAMA, HARI HARI. What is important here is not the meaning of the words but their actual sound and the movement of the breath and lips, giving direct experience of the basic energy of life as it comes from the void.

It is possible that in the course of contemplation there may arise visions or ecstatic states of consciousness, and it is a natural temptation to think of these as the goals of contemplation. However, to attempt to prolong these states, or to regain them when they subside, is like straining the facial muscles to see clearly, and is an effort to interrupt the natural flow of what is happening now. There may also arise a curious sensitivity to the unspoken thoughts and intentions of others, or astonishing dexterity of intellect or fidelity of memory, but these are not to be taken as signs of "progress" in contemplation, because contemplation ceases as soon as there is any seeking for results. Such temptations as these beset ritual contemplation in the same way as playing a musical instrument may be used for ends extraneous to the enjoyment of music, as in competing with oneself or with others for musical status.

Too much concern for ritual contemplation may also lead to a one-sidedly passive form of life and to the impression of falling away from the eternal now while engaged in other and more strenuous activities. Now, the habitual use of muscular tension as the referent for the ego in looking, listening, and willing carries over into the use of natural physical exertion in running, lifting, and hauling so as to make such actions seem entirely different from those which happen "of themselves," spontaneously. Curiously, this sets up, say, in the effort to run, a redundant effort to make the effort, giving the impression that the exertion of running is a direct demonstration of the activity and potency of the ego-image. We have learned, mostly as children, to put on an act of strenuousness while doing strenuous things. Yet efforts to make efforts, being redundant, work against the natural use of muscular energy in such a way that they are self-imposed obstacles, or efforts against effort. It is as if, in pulling, the triceps were to work against the biceps. When this redundant use of effort falls away, it becomes obvious

166

that decision to do this or that, and the consequent physical actions, happen of themselves like everything else.

Free action is certainly not caused by a purely abstract "I." It emerges from the total intelligence of the organism, in the same way as the growth of the brain and the digestion of food, and it will employ conscious reasoning in situations where reasoning is an appropriate tool. This would perhaps be called biologically or physically "determined" action by those who separate the organism from the rest of the universe, and see it "obeying" or "responding" to "drives" which have first been defined as external to itself. But the individual-and-universe has no external or extraneous determinant. The individual may be seen as constrained by natural processes only when viewed out of context as something *in* but not *of* its whole environment. Laws and artificial restraints become necessary when, through the illusion of separateness, the individual loses touch with his organic intelligence and feels at odds with his environment. Obviously, the operation of organic intelligence is not to be confused with the false spontaneity of actions deliberately calculated to be at variance with natural order or human law. Social conventions still govern those who go out of their way to oppose them.

In past times all matters concerning the practice of contemplation were considered esoteric or, what amounts in the West to the same thing, heretical—though not every heresy was of this order, and the contemplative way became heresy only as people tried to describe its content. For, speaking in religious language, it would be plain to the contemplative that only God exists and that there is nothing other than God. For obvious reasons this is a doctrine greatly feared by both ecclesiastical and secular rulers.

On the one hand, when it is necessary that the people be exploited and oppressed, it is important to imbue them with a servile mentality. On the other hand, when people are vulgar and greedy, the mere idea that "all is God" or that good and evil are polar is used to justify every wanton excess. It is for this reason that governments forbid the ingestion of hemp flowers and other psychedelic substances, lest immature and half-civilized individuals profane the mysteries. One does not wish noble wines to be used for drunken brawls.

The fiction of the isolated ego or person as the real individual has therefore been implanted to stimulate the feeling of creatureliness and the fear of God. It is likewise advantageous to rulers that the people be blind to the polarity of life and death, and so fear death if they fear not God. But when those who implant this fiction are also its dupes, they seek for themselves as persons the powers which they already enjoy as God, but have forgotten. In this endeavor they resort to such crude wisdom as may be expressed in linear signs, words, and numbers for the government of a nonlinear and immeasurably subtle world. And as the person is a linear version of man, confused with the real man, so the linear understanding of the world—with which linear wisdom must deal—is confused with the real world. Only by violence, then, can the real and living world be straightened out, squared away, evened off, boxed into clear-cut categories, and so conformed to the crudities of linear wisdom. Consequently, all the balances and interdependencies of nature are thrown into confusion—to the bewilderment of birds, beasts, and plants, and the befuddlement of man's own nonlinear body and brain. In such an emergency it is necessary to take the risks of exposing the illusion of the person and all its work, and to allow what has been esoteric to become generally known.

It is thus that, in contemplation, man discovers himself as inseparable from the cosmos as a whole in both its positive and negative aspects, its appearances and disappearances. Astronomy and physics are therefore theoretical adumbrations of the vastness of our dimensions, for it is not simply that we are subordinate *parts* of the system, but that the entire system is ourself in its full and only true sense. Ordinarily, we may glimpse this truth in a shallowly intellectual way, in affairs and basic emotions. But in contemplation this view is as real and self-evident as breathing and enables the problems of mundane life to be seen in their true perspective—*sub specie aeternitatis*—balancing and correcting the usual myopia of exclusive preoccupation with nasty little games and schemes.

Nature, that is, our own true nature, is bringing these preoccupations to a stop by coming forth with the technical power to pursue them on a colossal scale, hitherto unknown. Pursued and magnified with such power, they come swiftly to absurdity and catastrophe, so that their innate contradictions become obvious to all. For we have been trying to harness technology to the impossible game of having positive without negative, defying the principles of that very electricity upon which technology so largely depends. This objective is as illusory as the ego which seeks it.

Thus a time when the objective seems clearly unattainable is a time ripe for the unmasking of that ego—itself the persona-mask which conceals the splendor of our Original Face. When spring comes the buds break out of their husks, the little birds cast off their shells, and young plants burst from their seed-casings. When there is a crack in the Cosmic Egg, Buddha is about to be born.

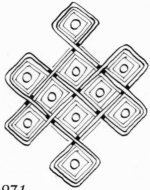

September 1, 1971

I have recently been studying G. Spencer Brown's book *Laws of Form* (Julian Press, New York, 1972), and though he was modest enough not to begin his title with the word *The*, this book is surely the most wonderful contribution to Western philosophy since Wittgenstein's *Tractatus*. This is not to be a review of it. I want to use the book as a point of departure for some further reflections. But it should be said, in passing, that this is a little classic of exquisite reasoning which goes down to the very roots of thinking, and could be called an approach to mystical experience by way of mathematical logic.

Spencer Brown explains that any universe is one turn, from the Latin *uni* (one) *vertere* (to turn). Now it's your turn. Every dog has its day. You have only one life. Thus a universe begins by drawing a distinction. You can make any distinction you like, but you must draw the line somewhere. But once you have done this, you set out on a path in which your choices are progressively limited and inevitable. When you were born, or conceived, you became one. But we

The Zero-One Amazement

171

don't know the meaning of one without none, and so one and none arrived together as the first distinction. We can say that before there was one there was none, though we should never have known this unless one had happened. But how could one come out of none? How did God create the universe out of nothing? To understand this you would have to have two turns instead of one. You would have to be able to turn, not just to the left or the right, but back upon yourself to see your own eyes.

This is like the ancient problem of being given three wishes. Be careful of what you desire: you may get it. The second wish has to be used, therefore, to cancel the first, because you will invariably regret an arbitrary and miraculous change in the course of nature when you behold its unforeseen results. The problem, which is like a Zen *koan*, is what to do with the third wish. We shall return to this in due course.

Spencer Brown's point is that a system which observes itself can never observe all of itself, and that, therefore, as our telescopes become more powerful the universe must necessarily expand. If I am continuous with the universe, if the physics of my body is the same as the physics of everything else, then I have the same relation to the outside world as to that much of my own body which I can see. Without mirrors I cannot see my back or my head. Even with mirrors I cannot see into my brain, and even if, like a neurosurgeon, I study other people's brains, I cannot study my own while I am doing it. This is utterly frustrating, but it has a marvelous and fascinating implication which is absolutely inescapable. You yourself are the universe which you are observing. You are trying to get at yourself when you love/hate other people. I am going to leave it to you

172

to work out the connection between the frustration and its implication (it's a wonderful trip), and only add that the aspect of yourself which you cannot see is obviously not any idea, image, or opinion of yourself that you have already formed.

So the first distinction is between none and one (or 0 and 1). This is the *yin* (negative) and *yang* (positive) polarity of the *Book of Changes*, which Leibnitz read in a Latin translation, and which gave him the idea that all numbers could be represented by the figures 0 and 1, so that for the series 1, 2, 3, 4, 5 we have 001, 010, 100, 101, 110, etc., which is now the arithmetic used by digital computers.

Therefore almost any information can be represented in these terms. Just as colored television is transmitted by nothing more than a series of pulses, all the information in our nervous systems is represented in terms of neuron cells which either respond or do not respond. The principle of the thing becomes obvious when you consider that sufficiently small dots and spaces of the same size can be arranged so as to represent any black-and-white photograph. This is a language. This same language can be used to inform a machine to select any one of four different colors when it prints a dot, thus it doesn't require too much imagination to see that all sensations and concepts can be conveyed, as on magnetic tape, in terms of nothing but *yang* dots and *yin* spaces. There is even a method whereby magnetic tape, which delivers or does not deliver a pulse (*yang*), can inform a machine using laser beams to sculpture any three-dimensional image from a block of plastic. So the question arises: If, given sufficient technical skill, we can reproduce everything that we can know in terms of a code consisting only of patterns of yes and no, on and off, are we simply reproducing what is already, and has always been, going on in the world?

This same question can be asked in a surprisingly different form: If we could attain perfect control of all events, would we not discover to our astonishment that we were doing what has always been happening?

This would involve, furthermore, the realization that what we had hitherto regarded as external and independent events were in fact our own behavior. Put it another way: If everything which happens is inevitable, this is only an obverse way of saying that we ourselves are doing it. A truly consistent fatalist will be forced to the conclusion that he is God and therefore has complete freedom of will. This is the principle of bending to survive and stooping to conquer. Calvinists (i.e., predestinarian Presbyterians) and Muslims half believe this. They concede that everything which comes to pass is the divine will, but continue to regard themselves as separate and submissive subjects of that will. They are therefore notably energetic and aggressive people, but because they still regard themselves as puppets of that will, their energy takes a divisive, cantankerous, hostile, and exclusive course. For when you surrender to God, you must secretly hate him and then vent this hatred on other people. But among Muslims there is a "heresy" called Sufism, and the Sufis know that there is no separate self to surrender to God: there is only God, Allah —upon which it is impossible to resist the play of words, "All . . . Ah!" So the Sufis say, "As there is no deity but he, there is no *he*ity [i.e., identity] but he." And it so happens that the Sufis represent the other side of Islam—not the dreary Koran and its raging prophetism, but music, dancing, and arabesques—all of which are patterns of conviviality.

174

Let us suppose, then, that you are suddenly struck with this realization that there is no "you" apart and separate from all that there is/isn't (for we must include the 0 as well as the 1, and for the same reason, we must include the death aspect as well as the life aspect, for you would not know that you were alive unless you had once been dead). The realization is at once thrilling and scary, like when we first came into being and made the distinction of deciding to be one. This is how Spencer Brown describes it:

> The skin of a living organism cuts off an outside from an inside. . . . By tracing the way we represent such a severance, we can begin to reconstruct, with an accuracy and coverage that appear almost uncanny, the basic forms underlying linguistic, mathematical, physical, and biological science, and can begin to see how the familiar laws of our own experience follow inexorably from the original act of severance. The act is itself already remembered, even if unconsciously, as our first attempt to distinguish different things in a world where, in the first place, the boundaries can be drawn anywhere we please. At this stage the universe cannot be distinguished from how we act upon it, and the world may seem like shifting sand beneath our feet.

As also when you listen to a recording of your own voice that comes back to you a second or so after you speak, you wait for that other fellow to go on. For we are accustomed to the feeling that the world is firmly ordained and constituted by someone or something other than ourselves, and thus an experience in which "the universe cannot be distinguished from how we act upon it" may be weirdly unnerving.*

* It is precisely this sensation which gives the horrors to people undergoing premature experiences of cosmic consciousness as a result of using LSD-25, or other psychedelic chemicals, without adequate intellectual preparation.

The cultures deriving from the Jewish, Christian, and Islamic religions are founded on this fear. "The fear of the Lord is the beginning of wisdom." They want to feel driven along looking, not straight ahead, but at the rear-vision mirror, following the commandments of their ancestors. Among these peoples it is therefore the greatest taboo, sin, and blasphemy to find out that the universe cannot be distinguished from how you act upon it—that you are, in fact, just as much an incarnation of God as Jesus or Kabir or Ramana Maharshi. But this is a state of nature, like having a heart, and is one of those things which (as Spencer Brown puts it)

> once they are discovered, are seen to be extremely simple and obvious, and make everybody, including their discoverer, appear foolish for not having discovered them before. It is all too often forgotten that the ancient symbol for the prenascence (i.e., prior to emergence state) of the world is a fool, and that foolishness, being a divine state, is not a condition to be either proud or ashamed of.

This is why, in the Buddhist cultures of the Far East, it is possible to have a popular Buddha who is a fat slob and an aimlessly wandering bum, Hotei, who carries a big bag of interesting rubbish which he gives away to children. (It is said that he was an eccentric Zen priest of the late T'ang dynasty. In twentieth-century America or the People's Republic of China he would be arrested as a vagrant lunatic and confined in a mental hospital.) For Hotei knows what to wish on the third—which is to wish not to wish any more. For when you see that the universe cannot be distinguished from how you act upon it there is neither fate nor free will, self nor other. There is simply one all-inclusive Happening, in which your personal sensation of being alive occurs in just the same way as the river flowing and the stars shining far out in space. There is no question of submitting or accepting or going with it, for what happens in and as you is no different from what happens as it. To think of submission is to divide yourself from it, and also to pile up a huge store of negative and aggressive energy against it.

This Happening may be called God, or the Tao, or the All-ah! You may even think of it as a conscious being, but if so, do not place upon it the burden and the bore of holding perpetual court to be flattered, petitioned, whined at, wheedled, apologized to, and howled at with hymns. Saint Paul ordered that women should be silent in church, but he himself prayed without ceasing. If you were Jesus, wouldn't you have turned to him and said, "Can't you be quiet for a while?"

To abandon the idea of separation from and submission to God has always been feared as a threat to morals, but there is absolutely no evidence to show that monotheists have behaved more lovingly to one another than pantheists. If anything, the evidence goes the other way, for all peoples who have a cosmology that corresponds to a military chain of command are obnoxious fighters and imperialists. They are forever punishing and disciplining other people for their own good, and milking them to the limit at the same time. And despite their professed atheism, Russia and China are both theocratic states, with icons and holy scriptures and inquisitions—except that their icons are enormous and vulgar photographs instead of sensitive paintings adorned with goldwork and jewels.

If a human being is to have dignity, serenity, and sanity —like a great tree, a lion, or a galaxy—he must understand and feel that he himself is, basically, this whole Happening and that his individual organism is one of its innumerable gestures. I said earlier that that aspect of yourself which you cannot see, which you cannot observe as an object, is not any idea, image, or opinion of yourself that you have formed or can ever form. But this is why Moses and Mohammed knew, in a rather obscure way, that one should not make images of God. Like a flawless crystal or lens, emptiness makes form perfectly clear, and this is why space—of which one is aware without being able to form an image of it—is the nearest we can get to an idea of God, and also to an apprehension of one's own unseen aspect.

A most curious consequence follows. As transparency, or emptiness, lends clarity and definition to form, I find that the more I understand that I myself am the Happening, and can make no mistake, the more I appreciate every kind of careful and formal discipline and technique. You are somehow freed to do things lovingly and well when you realize that you are not doing anything out of duty or obligation to an overlord. When you no longer make the distinction between the universe and how you are acting upon it, you are really on your own and so acquire a sense of responsibility. And to the degree that we develop (or that there grows in us) this sense of compassionate, as distinct from anxious, carefulness we shall be able to do without the State just as we have been learning to do without the Church.

The Seven Secret Sayings of God

Before [a]the beginning when God created the heaven and the earth, and the earth was without form, and void: and darkness was upon the face of the deep, God said [b]I AM THAT. And it is so.

2 Also, being in eternity which is neither linear nor sequential, where all is nowever, God said, YOU MUST DRAW THE LINE SOMEWHERE. And it was drawn.

3 But it was no dreary straight line or flat wall, for God then said, HAVE A BALL. And there was a ball, in the image whereof all stars and planets came to be formed.

4 Thereupon God said, THERE ARE TWO SIDES TO EVERYTHING. And there are: the inside and the outside, the dense and the spacious, the right and the wrong, the left and the taken, for, as it is written, [c]One shall be taken, and the other left.

5 And God said, IT MUST BE IN TIME. And thereafter it was, is, and will be, for as it is written again, [d]As it was in the beginning is now, and ever shall be, through all ages of ages. Amen.

6 And forthwith God said, SPACE IT OUT. Whereupon it came to pass that, beside this and that and now and then, there is also here and there.

7 And God beheld [e]how firm a foundation this was and said unto himself, GET LOST. And there you are.

a Gen. 1.1-2.
Ps. 33.6.
Acts. 14.15

b Ex. 3.14.
Jno. 8.58

c Mat. 24.40-41

d Lit.St. John
Chrys.

e Hymn 564.